Attitude

Ted Rall

TeoPhi

Attitude

The New Subversive Political Cartoonists

NANTIER · BEALL · MINOUSTCHINE
Publishing inc.
new york

Also available:
Attitude 2, $13.95
with Keith Knight, Neil Swaab, Emily S. Flake,
Tak Toyoshima, Brian Sendelbach, Jennifer
Berman, Alison Bechdel, Shannon Wheeler,
Mikhaela B. Reid, Aaron McGruder, Tim Kreider,
Barry Deutsch, David Rees, Max Cannon, Eric
Orner, Greg Peters, Jason Yungbluth, Stephen
Notley, Justin Jones, Kevin Moore, Marian Henley

Acknowledgments

*Special thanks are due to my wife without whom the Herculean task of
collecting, formatting and sorting a thousand cartoons and other images would never have
gotten done. Fellow cartoonist and illustrator J.P. Trostle designed and art-directed this book to
great effect for little remuneration; thanks for a labor of love. I relied on the following people
for advice and support: Ruben Bolling, Ted Keller, Peter Kuper, Ray Lesser, my mom,
Martin Satryb, Bill Smith, Cole Smithey, Ward Sutton, Bill Taylor, Tom Tomorrow.
Finally, thanks to Terry Nantier at NBM for taking yet another chance.*

Editor: **Ted Rall**

Art Director: **J.P. Trostle**

Contents page photo by: **Ross Taylor**

We have over 150 titles; write
for our color catalog:
NBM
555 Eighth Ave., Suite 1202
New York, NY 10018
see our website at www.nbmpublishing.com
5   4
Library of Congress Control Number: 2002106997
ISBN 1-56163-317-8
This anthology is Copyright © 2002 Ted Rall.

Contents

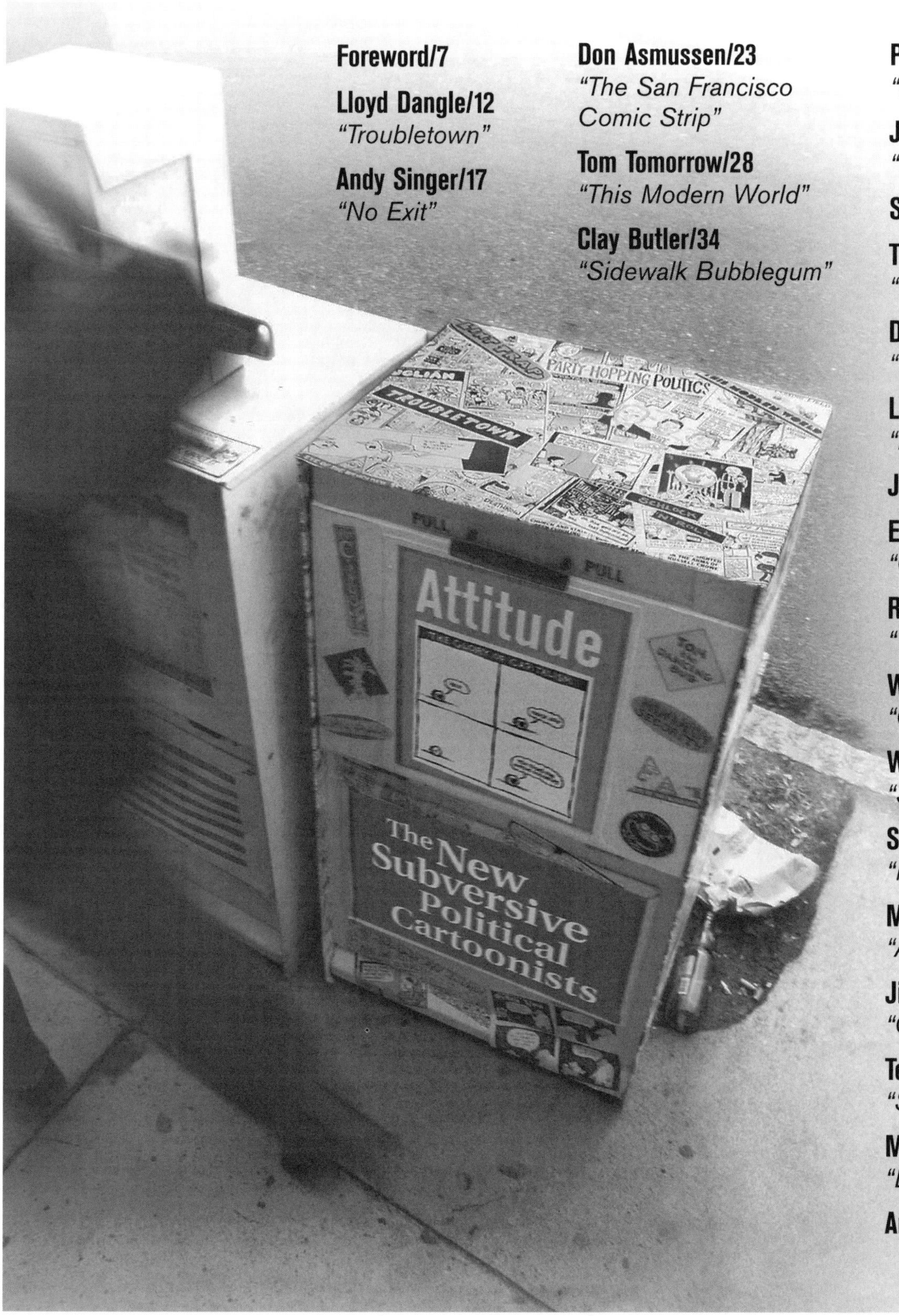
TROUBLETOWN
PARTY-HOPPING POLITICS
PULL
PULL
Attitude
The New Subversive Political Cartoonists

Foreword

Ted Rall tells you why you're reading this book

"The people interviewed in this book are not 'pop,' as in the widely-recognized popularity and visibility of a Sinatra or a Warhol. But neither are they 'underground' — as in unknown — figures either, although they once were." — *Introduction to Notes from the Pop Underground, by Peter Belsito, 1985*

Cartoonists and their fans like to divide comics into two distinct categories: mainstream and underground. Comic strips that appear in daily newspapers, like "The Family Circus," "The Wizard of Id" and "Apartment 3-G," are mainstream. Underground comics feature words and imagery that editors of daily papers believe would provoke floods of angry letters; they're defined simply by *not* being mainstream. Underground comics can enjoy spectacular success, even getting turned into big-time movies, while many mainstream comic strips languish without ever achieving commercial viability, much less actual profitability. In the end, it's all about content; like porn, you know underground comics when you see them.

Unlike porn, not enough people see them.

Mickey Siporin

This anthology is the first attempt to bring together a genre of cartoonists—to be specific, political cartoonists—who can be classified in neither (or both) of the above phyla. Too alternative for the mainstream and too mainstream for the underground, the artists in this book tend to fall between the cracks of our narrowly-segmented mass-market culture. Their drawing styles and narrative approaches cover a huge range, yet they have a lot in common.

These alternative weekly political cartoonists draw in styles variously described as edgy, rough, different, amateurish, disturbing, scratchy, dark, striking and incompetent. Unlike their colleagues on the editorial pages of the nation's chain-owned daily newspapers who produce empty jokes about the news, these men and women revel in anger about issues that matter to ordinary people. They name names. They ridicule their readers as much as their leaders. They tend to be concerned about similar issues: commercialism, global warming, free trade, alienation, the two-party system. And in the proudest traditions of great art and political activism, they're not drawing these cartoons for the money. Cartooning won't change the world, but that's no reason not to try.

Tim Eagan

Political cartooning as we know it—mainstream political cartooning—is a dying craft. Democratic donkeys and Republican elephants still prowl a hundred drafting tables and every city in America awakens to tortured analogies on the op-ed page—ships piloted by president-as-captain going down in a sea labeled "deficit," anyone?—but there are fewer old-school edit-toon guys, and those who remain are doing work of increasing banality every year. Editorial cartoonists are getting fired like they're going out of style because they *are* out of style. Newspaper consolidation and closures have cost countless cartoonists their jobs, but the sad fact is that readers have become too sophisticated for those 19th century donkeys and elephants. Most editorial cartoonists draw in cross-hatched styles directly de-

rived from Jeff MacNelly and Pat Oliphant's mid-'60s epoch; is it any shock that what worked against LBJ doesn't cut it now?

I began cartooning in earnest in 1987. After collecting two shoe boxes full of rejection letters from daily newspaper editors, in a desperate gambit to get exposure, I resorted to taping Xerox copies of my work to lamp posts and bus stops in New York City. Now and then, a letter from the editor of a small publication interested in publishing my stuff would appear in my post office box. Eventually, I heard from the art director of a new alternative weekly paper in Manhattan, *NY Perspectives*. Although my cartoons now run in dailies as well as weeklies, such free-distribution weeklies as *The Village Voice* and *Sacramento News & Review* are infinitely more responsive to the

Peter Kuper

Lloyd Dangle

kind of work I do. Weekly editors don't think that there's any one way to draw comics. They run your cartoons every week, in the same spot, so their readers develop an intimate relationship with your work. Their readers skew younger and smarter than the dailies. And nobody worries that a few naughty words will inspire some old lady to cancel her subscription.

Of course, I 'm not alone. Most of the other cartoonists in these pages got their start during the late '80's and '90's in the pages of alternative weeklies, often deeply buried in the classifieds and porn ads. Almost all of them consider the weeklies their spiritual home. After all, the weeklies themselves are often too mainstream for the underground and too underground to be mainstream.

I make no claim to impartiality on this subject but I nonetheless submit that alternative political comics may be the only truly relevant form of cartooning today. Contemporary "underground" cartooning is profoundly influenced by two seminal sources: Robert Crumb's neurotic psychosexual navel-gazing and the art-school pretension of the 1980's. The latter espouses the Joycean notion that readers should work as hard to understand as artists toil to create; valid or not, few comics consumers possess the inclination or the desire to do so. While art comics collect awards and critical acclaim, they're read by a tiny minority and understood by a still-smaller subset of that elitist group.

Intelligent art is rarely popular. Nevertheless, even the snottiest artist understands that he or she is nothing without an audience. Cartoonists like Ruben Bolling and Tom Tomorrow make every possible concession to commercial viability—straightforward panel-by-panel structures and narrative styles lifted from "Peanuts," for instance—without compromising

Scott Bateman

their vision of the world or the possibilities presented by a blank sheet of paper. You don't have to own the collected works of Derrida to "get" their work, but you come away with a hell of a lot more than a quick guffaw about Bill, Monica and a tasty Cohiba.

Unlike the art-school crowd, the altie artists in *Attitude* attempt to engage ordinary people by presenting new ideas with words and pictures that any-

Tom Tomorrow

Ward Sutton

Lalo Alcaraz

Don Asmussen

Bill Brown

body can understand. That's why these cartoonists have also appeared in such middle-of-the-road publications as *Rolling Stone, TV Guide, Time* and *Newsweek.* But populism doesn't have to mean dumbing-down. If some people can't deal with so many words and so many rough edges, so be it.

I have attempted to make this book as comprehensive as possible. Creators were selected for their commitment to alternative-weekly-based political cartooning; you'll find both well-established and nascent talents in these pages. Other weekly comics, important though they may be, were not included because they either didn't contain enough overtly political commentary or because I wasn't aware of them. To this latter group: sorry.

I am indebted to Andrea Juno's 1997 book *Dangerous Drawings* for inspiring this book's format. Though cartoons can and should speak for themselves, my hope is that the interviews and personal ephemera accompanying each artist's work will help contextualize their visions more effectively. Most of all, however, I offer my thanks to the 20 other cartoonists who gave up their precious time and energy to share themselves and their work.

TED RALL

Eric Bezdek

Lloyd Dangle

Trouble is Lloyd Dangle's business – and business is good

"Troubletown" by Lloyd Dangle reads like a roller-coaster; his loose style and conversational tone makes it essential to the readers of the *San Francisco Bay Guardian*, Seattle's *The Stranger*, and *Miami New Times*. Based in Oakland, California, the 41-year-old Dangle is well-known as a major underground comics artist and illustrator.

TED RALL: You're obviously a very angry man. Most of the cartoonists in this book are either very angry men or very angry women and most of them trace their anger to some seminal experience in their lives. What pissed you off so damn much? Did you grow up poor? Divorced parents? What?

LLOYD DANGLE: This will be disappointing, but I'm not really that angry. My father was angry when he was younger and used to kick our dog but that didn't scar me for life. I learned from him that having a job you can't stand causes you to walk around with smoke coming out of your ears, and I knew at a very young age that I would

avoid that. I decided that I would try to make a job out of drawing funny pictures. Of course, I still have smoke coming out of my ears some days, it's genetically hard-wired, but, most of the time, I'm pretty happy. Being a cartoonist is very satisfying.

Part of the reason there is anger in my cartoons is simply because I like to pump emotion into my characters, and irritability is a funny, funny emotion. I like characters who are paralyzed with anger, and a lot of people apparently know the feeling. Like the guy in San Jose who recently stood trial for throwing a poodle [actually, a bichon frissé] onto the freeway while in the midst of a road rage attack—he's definitely the kind of person we see in "Troubletown".

Tom Tomorrow portrays business executives as cogs in the corporate machine, I draw them as clueless dolts and you view them as rabidly hostile white men who see themselves as hopelessly misunderstood. Why do we have such a dim view of business people?

People desperately want to be good, and admired for being good, but they also want to be

Lloyd Dangle in 1989 when Troubletown began. Does this man look angry?

rich. These things rarely fit together. Honest investors who study the market realize that stocks with the highest rates of return are the ones that cause the most evil to humanity. This conflict makes business people human and funny. The rabid hostility comes from defensiveness and you can read it in the newspapers every day. Business executives must justify their place in a world where the stock market shoots up on the announcement of thousands of workers being fired. This creates a lot of irritability and confusion for my poor white male characters.

One of my most popular cartoons was one in which two women are sitting at a kitchen table talking about a recent career move one of them had made. As the strip continues, you realize she is a dominatrix, because every so often she gets up and kicks and abuses a naked white man who is cleaning her floor with his toothbrush. She feels good about what she's doing but, in the end, the guy is paying her and says, "good, now I can go destroy some more old-growth forests." I know people related to it because the mail from dominatrixes and dominatrix clients came pouring in.

If you could wave your magic wand and create any economic system you wanted, what would you conjure up?

Income tax would be progressive (really progressive with corporations kicking in, not like the way it is now); there'd be no sales tax. Gambling taxes (including on the stock market) would fund schools and municipal services (like in Nevada, only better) and the Library of Congress would institute a copyright licensing system that would make it so cartoonists' bank accounts would fill up automatically without us ever having to collect from deadbeats.

Nowadays, there's a big debate in the cartooning community over the importance of craft, especially as it relates to drawing ability. What's more important to a successful cartoon, in your opinion—the words or the pictures?

I'm so glad I don't get involved in cartoonist debates! The combination of drawing to writing is individual to every cartoonist and that's what's great about it. Everybody takes a different road. If you're lucky, you hit upon the right combination and you find your voice. Then you hang on to what works and hope it pays.

You've never won any major awards for your work, which surprises me given the respect you enjoy among comics fans and others. Do you just not apply for them or is there some other reason

you get passed over? And are awards bullshit or are winners an accurate reflection of the best in any given field?

Thanks, Ted. I've never applied for any awards in cartooning or illustration, but this year a cartoon I did for *Sierra Magazine* got nominated for a Maggie Award. I haven't heard if I won. Damn, I was probably passed over again! I've never believed any awards are really fairly judged and I don't really care about them. It's stupid, I know, because having won some awards would be good for promotional purposes. I could use a Pulitzer right now.

In a cartoon you did about the Napster controversy, you portray disgruntled Metallica fans as ungrateful thieves. Have you ever discovered that someone was running or reproducing your work without obtaining your permis-

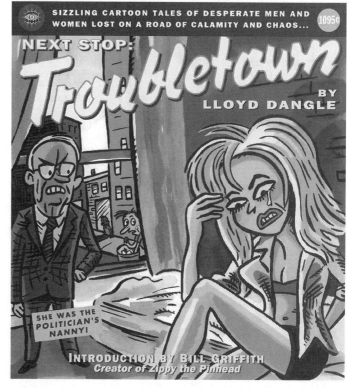

sion? If so, did you take legal action against them?

I meant to portray the Metallica fans as self-righteous consumers, who feel so entitled to get free stuff that they can't imagine it could be wrong. I got so many e-mails about that cartoon! The tortured logic they use! "Mick Jagger is so rich, he doesn't deserve any more of my money," was a common argument.

I have discovered people reproducing

my stuff without permission a couple of times but the only action I took was writing letters to them telling them to stop. I register all of my work with the copyright office so I have the ability to go after infringers for statutory damages. The people who infringed me were just too clueless and pathetic for me to want to hurt them financially. I hope at least I taught them something.

Some of your cartoons mix the more arcane aspects of economics, journalism and politics. Do you get complaints that your work is too complex for the average reader? Which gets us into: are most people dumb?

The stuff that I write about is exactly what appears in the news and on TV but twisted around a bit. I don't pretend to be a professor of economics or anything, I just make fun of the anecdotes and justifications you hear in public discourse. Even though my cartoons sometimes cause controversy, they never have any more sex or profanity than TV shows at 8 pm. I don't think people are dumb but if they are it's not my problem. I write cartoons to please myself, or someone with my level of intelligence and sense of humor—and I'm no rocket scientist.

E-mails I receive from disgruntled readers indicate to me that many people lack basic writing skills and the ability to build a logical argument. But otherwise they seem very smart.

You live in the East Bay of San Francisco. Why do people drive so incredibly slowly there? I've seen quicker reaction times in Florida retirement communities.

I live in Oakland. My experience is different because I live on a crack dealer drag strip, and crack makes drivers more peppy. The local NIMBY ["Not In My Back Yard"] group petitioned for speed bumps, which now causes loud, scraping thump noises every time a car bottoms out at 60 miles per hour. It's possible you were living in an aged hippie community where there is a high use of medical marijuana. Things tend to go at a slower pace.

What do you think of mainstream editorial cartoonists, with their donkeys and elephants, labels and analogies? Would you describe American political cartooning as vibrant, moribund or somewhere in between?

I think the lame political cartoons mirror our lame political system. I've actually done some lobbying in California for artists' issues and it's so dull watching these folks [politicians] boil every issue down to a basic partisan position. "Oh, I am a Republican so I must behave like this." "I am a good Democrat so I must behave like this."

Tom Toles is brilliant. The only other one I really pay attention to is Oliphant, just because he's everywhere. Oliphant is fun to watch because every three weeks or so he gives in to his horrible retrograde tendency of using old racial stereotypes, like big buck-toothed Chinamen and such. A few of his Greenspan cartoons were greedy Jew stereotypes that got the Anti Defamation League pissed off. He's like the Charlton Heston of cartooning. You never know what kind of nutty thing he'll do next.

What cartoon have you done that has gotten the most reaction?

The Napster ones. The youth accused me of being a corporate sellout on the RIAA payroll, which I enjoyed, even though it's not true.

When you were in high school, were you popular?

I guess I was sort of popular because I could draw funny pictures and the creeps were fascinated by that. But I was withdrawn and had low self-esteem so I was always on the outside.

Lloyd Dangle, far left, wants you to know that he grew up as a redneck in Michigan.

Lloyd Dangle

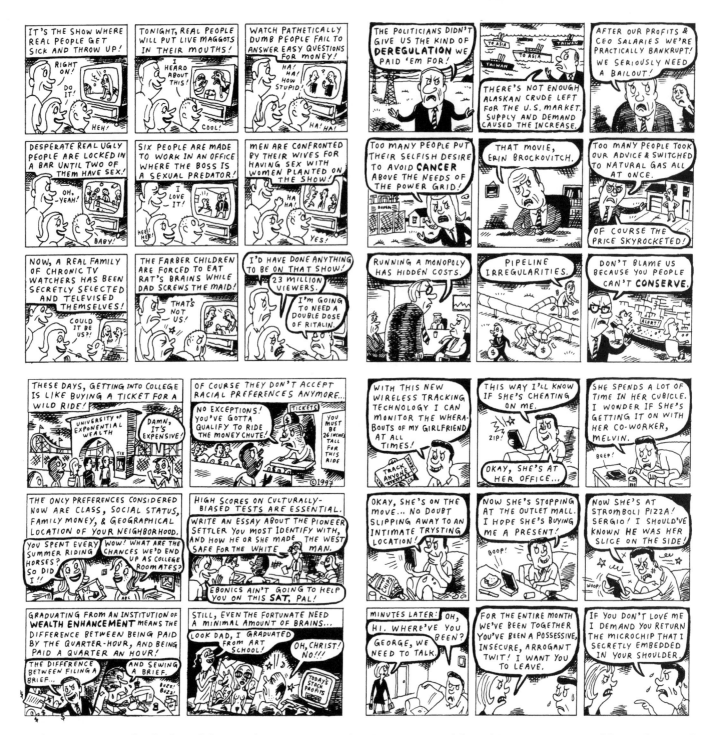

Did you go to art school? If so, did you like it? Should aspiring cartoonists go to art school?

I went to the University of Michigan school of art. Art school is useful in developing a shield of pompousness and false confidence which is necessary for any artistic pursuit. Also, this is where you make contact with the heirs and heiresses to great family fortunes who may hire you and float you when you're struggling. You may get access to inspirational artwork in the libraries and museums that you might not otherwise happen upon, and it gives you a model of what a working artist looks like, which otherwise would be completely outside of normal experience. Other than that, I can't name anything specific about cartoons I learned, other than that my professors didn't like them.

If you could do anything you wanted and live anywhere you wanted, what would you do and where would you go?

Every time I go on vacation I tell my wife, I want to live here! Then we always go back to Oakland and I forget about it. Things are pretty good here. If I moved to Hawaii, what would I draw comics about? Sunburn Town? Mahi-Mahi Town? I'd really be at a loss.

Andy Singer

For this cynic, there's "No Exit" until we wise up

Appearing in a handful of papers, Andy Singer's "No Exit" succeeds where dozens of Pulitzer Prize-winning political cartoonists fail every day: it makes strong statements in a single panel. And look—no cheesy labels! Singer, 36, is more interested in systems than personalities; he's particularly obsessed with car culture and its effect on the environment, as well as self-alienation. Among alternative cartoons, his work is especially notable for its iconic graphics. "No Exit" appears regularly in *Funny Times, Carbusters* and *Z* magazine and has also been published in such mainstream venues as *The New Yorker.*

TED RALL: It seems like I see your work everywhere—*Funny Times, Comic Relief,* T-shirts. So what's this about you not making lots of money from your cartoons?

ANDY SINGER: For one thing, I only appear regularly in 10-to-12 publications. It takes at least 30 to make a decent living. I'm not sure why I've never been able to get published in more places. In part I think it's because my cartoons aren't focused enough at a particular audience. They're too alternative and political for daily papers but not quirky or wordy enough for alternative weeklies. The fact that I'm a terrible businessman doesn't help matters either. I hate selling myself to people. In the last two years, however, I have made more of an effort to do this. Hopefully, it will pay off.

You're interested in the mechanics of power. Have you ever considered running for political office yourself?

Primarily, I'm interested in the

mechanics of power so that, through my art, I can expose how it functions. I've thought about running for office, but even getting a seat on a city council requires a ton of connections and a lot of money. In the end, I'm a much better artist than a politician, so I've contented myself with working for other people whose views I like. In addition to voting, I've collected signatures, written letters and editorials, phone-banked, raised money, donated money and physically protested and supported many different candidates and ideas. I've done a lot of free illustration for non-profit causes, which I also consider a form of activism, and I try to bring my political views into my cartoons.

Your strip being called "No Exit," the obvious question of a Sartrian influence on your work seems self-evident. Are you an existentialist, or are you waiting for a payoff beyond the grave?

No, I don't think there's some "personal payoff beyond the grave" but I do believe in Karma—that what you do has an effect on other people even after you die. As far as the existentialists go, I like Albert Camus

more than Sartre. I only first read Sartre's play "No Exit" two or three years ago and found it kind of cold and negative.

Camus has a lot more love and passion. In "The Fall," he argues that heaven and hell are right here on earth, that "The Last Judgment" occurs every day, and that the most basic choice you have is whether or not to kill yourself. If you choose to live, then you must embrace life and fight death in all its personal and social manifestations.

I choose to live, so I am against cultural and environmental suicide. Our society is suicidal. You see this in people's eating and living habits, in the way we consume resources and in the way we are destroying our environment and each other. We need to confront this, since there is no escape—"No Exit." That's partly where the name for my cartoon comes from. Mainly it is just a reference to confronting and making light of the difficult aspects of life.

Many political cartoonists are interested in the role of the automobile in American society, epitomized most recently by the rise of the nine mile-per-gallon SUV and its devastating effect on the environment. But you've made car culture something of an obsession. Why is that? Did you get hit by a car when you were a kid?

No, nothing terrible has happened to me, though I have lost a few friends in car crashes over the years. But I think everyone knows a few people who've died or been severely injured by cars. My obsession with cars is based on my obsession with the environment.

Food, housing and transportation are the three big human and environmental issues. That's where most of our resources go and where most of our pollution is generated. The first issue (food) is heavily dealt with. You've got Frances Moore Lappé and *Food First*, the whole organics movement, *Fast Food Nation*, opposition to genetic engineering, etc.

The second issue is dealt with also, at least somewhat, in that we are beginning to talk about development, sprawl, energy efficiency, the use of tropical hardwoods and other endangered materials.

Transportation, however, is the big elephant in the bedroom that no one

wants to seriously discuss. In the U.S., "transportation" means cars. America has three times more registered motor vehicles than licensed drivers. We are a nation in love with cars and we are pushing this car-oriented transportation model on the rest of the world. In 10 years, the world's motor vehicle population is projected to top one billion.

Cars are environmental enemy number one. A third of all global warming gas comes directly from automobile tailpipes. If you include the pollution generated in their manufacture and disposal as well as the pollution created by the building of roads and highways, then cars are responsible for half of all global warming gas (as well as half of toxic air pollution and over a third of all smog). Cars (and the transportation sector) also consume half of all petroleum produced in the world...and

Andy's mask designs. He builds them, and other sculptural objects, out of recycled materials. He has exhibited and sold a few but mostly gives them out as gifts to friends.

account for the pressure to drill for oil in the Alaskan National Wildlife Refuge and other sensitive areas. One million vertebrate animals (including many endangered species) are killed on U.S. roads every day.

Cars suck up a fifth of Americans' personal incomes and billions of our tax dollars. They destroy wilderness and farmlands with sprawl. They destroy cities with noise and smog. They are responsible for tire fires, water pollution, toxic waste disposal problems, tanker spills, wars fought for oil, the continued export of leaded gasoline to Eastern Europe and the developing world and a host of other problems. The list is endless.

Big environmental groups sometimes talk about greenhouse gasses from cars and occasionally link them to sprawl and other problems, but, primarily, they focus on land preservation and policing industry. We should have an international environmental organization devoted entirely to combating cars and sprawl. It could lobby for moratoriums on new

> "Transportation is the big elephant in the bedroom that no one wants to discuss ... America has three times more registered motor vehicles than licensed drivers."

roads, stricter emissions standards, an end to highway subsidies, increased gas taxes, improved public transport, road pricing, better zoning laws, and much more. In the 1990's, smaller alternative transport groups have begun to spring up around the country. You are seeing "Critical Mass" bike rides and other forms of resistance to roads and sprawl and public support for mass transit.

Since no other artist seems to focus on this issue, I have taken it on myself. I try to provide the aforementioned groups with good images to help them get their message across to politicians and the public.

Come on, admit it: Driving can be a lot of fun, especially when it's not just a daily commute to and from a crappy job. Don't you enjoy driving just a bit?

I've never owned a car, yet I've driven so often (for work and others) that the magic of driving has completely worn off. I still enjoy riding in older cars (from

the "Golden Age" of driving). A friend of mine maintains a 1963 Buick Electra that is a joy to ride in...but new cars do nothing for me. They're piles of snaptogether, foul-smelling plastic. Besides, in this situation, it's not about what I enjoy. I could enjoy murdering people but hopefully, for its own good, society would prevent me from doing this. The only thing I like about cars is listening to "Car Talk" on NPR.

What exactly is your interest in Latin America and how does it impact your cartoons?

Self-portrait for "Funk"

I am interested in how European colonialists and the U.S. have manipulated and exploited Latin America for cheap labor and natural resources. I'm into learning about how the CIA backed a coup in Guatemala in 1954, or backed Augusto Pinochet's coup in Chile in 1973 (supported by Nixon and Kissinger).

I'm interested in U.S. military involvement in Haiti, Cuba, Nicaragua, Panama, Mexico, El Salvador and Columbia. I'm interested in the exploitation of the tropical rain forest (and near-elimination of this hemisphere's dry tropical forests), the use of dangerous pesticides outlawed in the U.S., the destruction of coral reefs, the rise of sweat shops and their links to free trade.

I am interested in all this stuff because I think it is critical to confront it if we want to survive as a planet. I try to work it into my cartoons, expose it and show connections.

If there were a revolution, would you be killed as an intellectual or lauded as an early proponent of social change?

I'd probably be killed, because I'm scrawny and not very well connected. I'm not an advocate of revolutions, at least not violent ones. They rarely solve anything. Often, the new group in power is just as awful as the old one.

What's your opinion of labeling in political cartoons? Most altie cartoonists don't use them, shunning them as mainstream, but you use them from time to time.

My goal is to get a message across, so I'll use whatever technique best accomplishes that. For me, the message is an important part of what makes a cartoon "alternative," not just the style. There are a lot of folks out there with nice styles who don't say shit.

Americans are living longer than before, yet their environment has never been dirtier. Paradox?

I don't totally agree. Many places in America are much cleaner than they were 40 or 50 years ago—like Pittsburgh, for instance, which used to have dozens of working steel mills and coal-burning trains blackening its skies. Now the trains burn diesel and the mills are gone—moved overseas to other countries. The Hudson and the Charles rivers (to name two) have been cleaned up considerably.

Hell, since they opened up the circulation pipes, you can actually see horseshoe crabs and egrets in the Gowanus canal (in Brooklyn, New York). Some rivers are worse, mainly due to agricul-

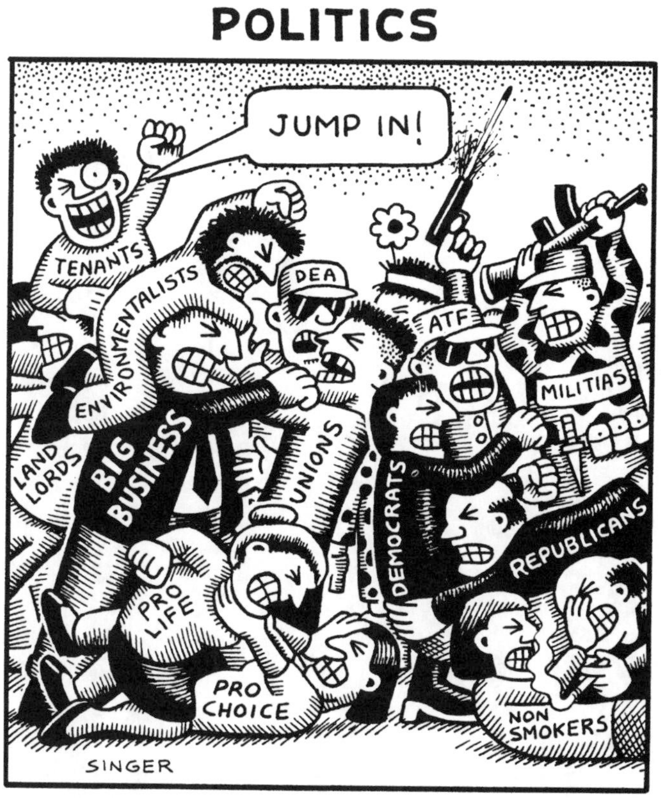
POLITICS
JUMP IN!
TENANTS
ENVIRONMENTALISTS
DEA
ATF
MILITIAS
LAND LORDS
BIG BUSINESS
UNIONS
DEMOCRATS
REPUBLICANS
PRO LIFE
PRO CHOICE
NON SMOKERS
SINGER

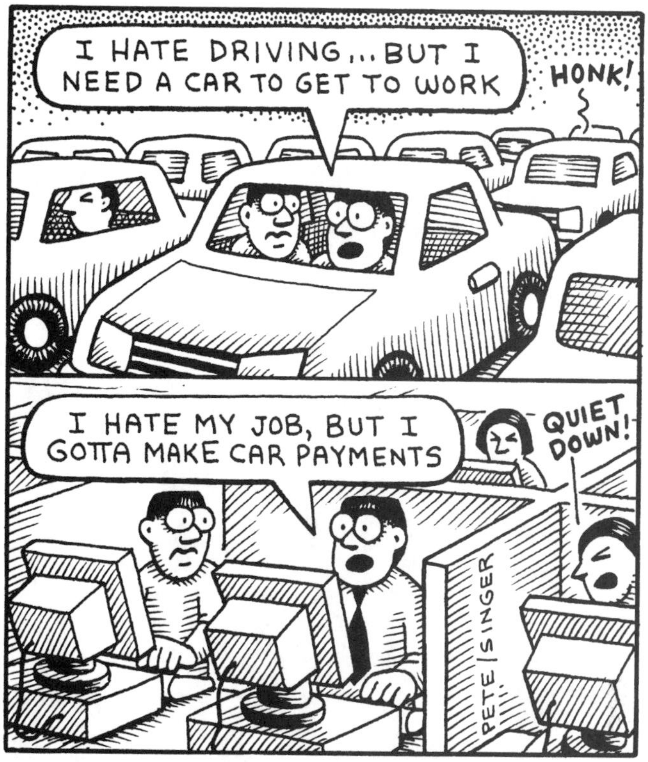
I HATE DRIVING... BUT I NEED A CAR TO GET TO WORK
HONK!
I HATE MY JOB, BUT I GOTTA MAKE CAR PAYMENTS
QUIET DOWN!
PETE SINGER

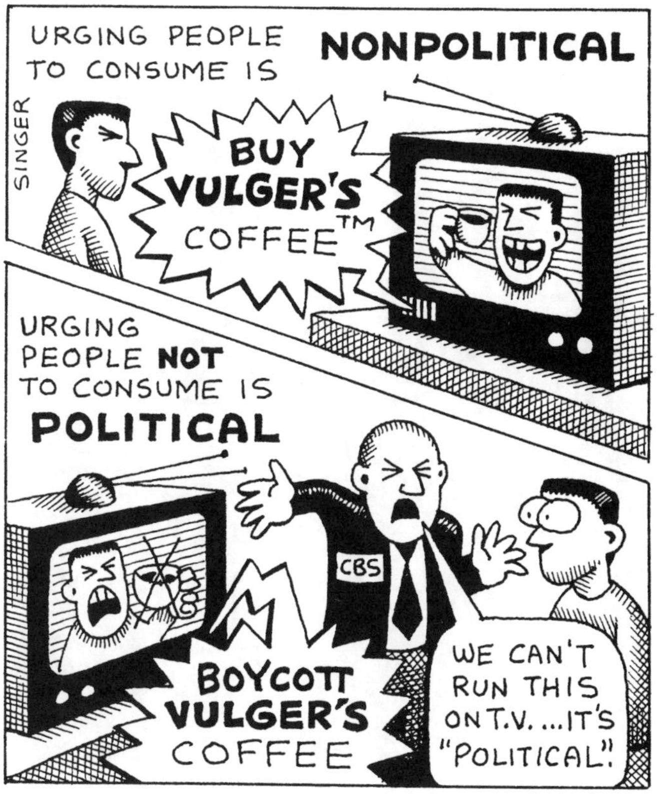
URGING PEOPLE TO CONSUME IS NONPOLITICAL
SINGER
BUY VULGER'S COFFEE™
URGING PEOPLE NOT TO CONSUME IS POLITICAL
CBS
BOYCOTT VULGER'S COFFEE
WE CAN'T RUN THIS ON T.V. ...IT'S "POLITICAL"!

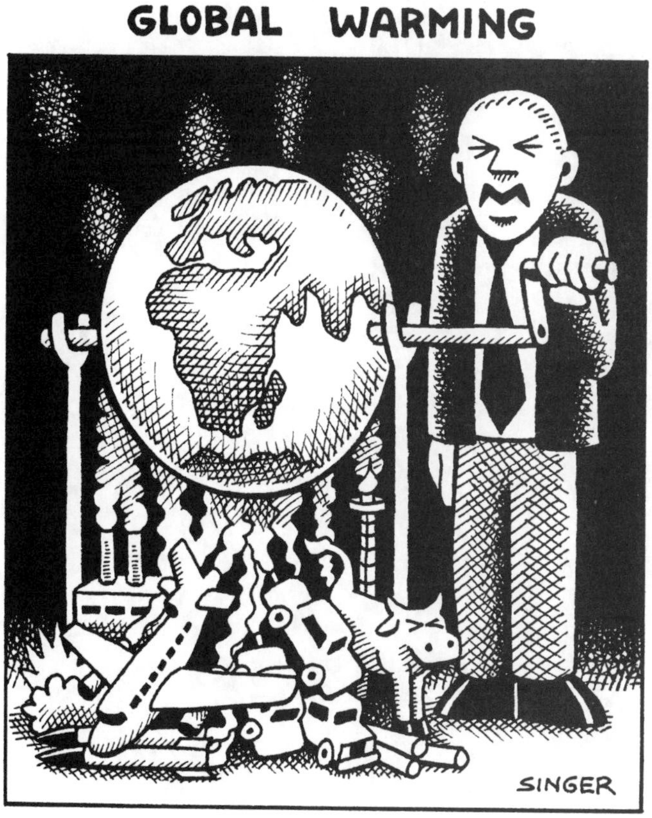
GLOBAL WARMING
SINGER

tural pesticide and livestock runoff, but mostly it's better. The sad part is, in many cases, we've just moved the pollution to Latin America and elsewhere and not really cleaned it up.

The major cause for the increase in Americans' life spans has been the increase in life-saving drugs and medical procedures. Sadly, the simplest of these drugs and procedures are not available to a huge part of the world who cannot afford them. So I would doubt that, globally, human life span has been significantly increased... but I don't know about this, so maybe I'm wrong.

Which network TV news do you prefer and why?

I don't own a television. If I did, I'd never get anything done.

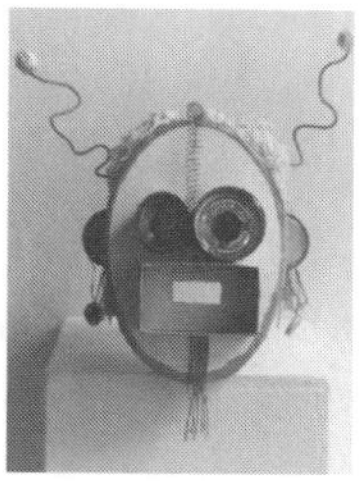

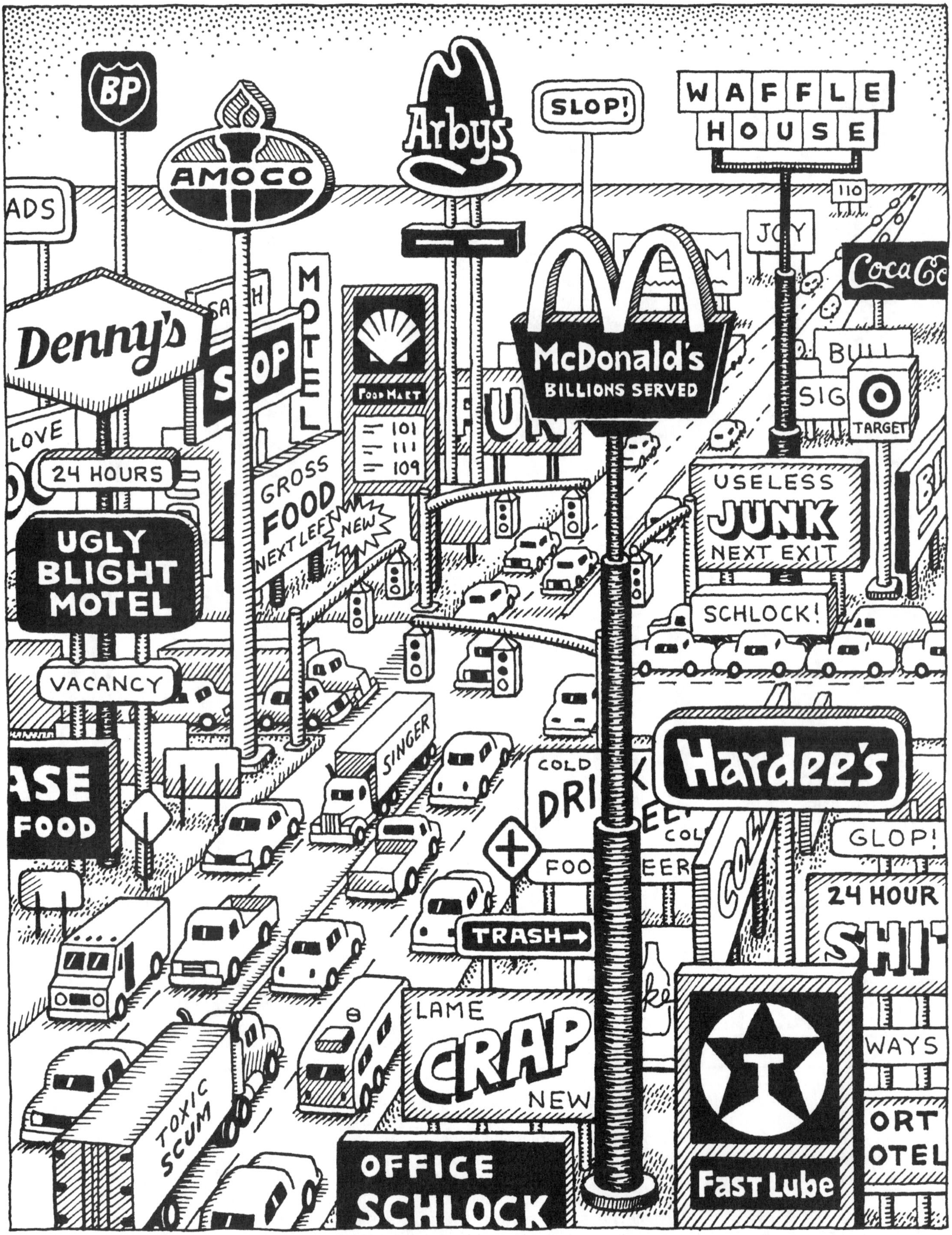
BP
AMOCO
Arby's
SLOP!
WAFFLE HOUSE
ADS
110
JOY
Coca Co
Denny's
SLOP
MOTEL
FOOD MART
101
111
109
McDonald's
BILLIONS SERVED
BULL
SIG
TARGET
FUN
LOVE
24 HOURS
GROSS FOOD NEXT LEFT
NEW
USELESS JUNK NEXT EXIT
UGLY BLIGHT MOTEL
SCHLOCK!
VACANCY
SINGER
Hardee's
ASE FOOD
COLD DRI
GLOP!
24 HOUR
SHIT
TRASH→
LAME CRAP NEW
WAYS
TOXIC SCUM
ORT
OTEL
OFFICE SCHLOCK
Fast Lube

Don Asmussen

A San Franciscan's hip twist on The Onion

Don Asmussen, 36, is the charming, joke-a-second creator of "The San Francisco Comic Strip." The strip runs in the *San Francisco Chronicle,* one of the nation's largest newspapers and originated in the now-defunct *San Francisco Examiner* (also a big daily paper, but one that ran alternative cartoons—oh, never mind). TSFCS serves as a quirky companion to Asmussen's more mainstream-oriented work for *Time* magazine. Though well-known for his type-laden headline parodies, he has won numerous illustration awards. Asmussen also worked on Henry Selick's animated film "MonkeyBone" and created/directed an animated Web show, "Like, News," for MondoMedia.

TED RALL: How did you first get into cartooning? How and when did "The San Francisco Comic Strip" begin?

DON ASMUSSEN: I didn't start cartooning professionally until 1995. Before that, I was an illustrator with a decidedly non-cartoony style, more of darker pen and ink/collage mix. I would do a lot of celebrity or political portraits for various magazines. I had put together a decent freelance career and was pretty happy, and *Communication Arts* magazine had just profiled my illustration work in '94, so that seemed to be my future.

Right after that profile, I was hired by *The San Francisco Examiner* in '95 as a full time illustrator. But then the paper's executive editor, Phil Bronstein [since famously married to actress Sharon Stone], saw some goofy cartoon scribblings I was doing as jokes for co-workers, thought they were funny, and put me on assignment to cover a local political debate in cartoon form. The reader reaction was huge, so I was converted to a weekly cartoonist immediately and the strip was named "The San Francisco Comic Strip" for lack of any better names. I haven't done illustration since.

"The San Francisco Comic Strip" is a rare member of a vanishing breed: The local-issue political cartoon, which is succumbing to newspaper consolidation and syndication. The fact that your work is done in an edgy, alternative style further separates it from common genre distinctions. Do you feel that your local work is more or less effective than your national cartoons for *Time* magazine?

What a wonderful thought, being part of a vanishing breed. Ouch. The strip did start out as a local-issue-only strip in '95, but in '96 I was assigned to cover the Democratic and GOP presidential conventions and that expanded the strip's scope. Now, it's a mix. I think doing national stories helps me get more readers, 'cause most younger readers don't care about the local supervisors' meetings.

I agree that there aren't too many strips that are local anymore. It's a cost thing. I'm lucky the *Examiner* wanted to be different. We were an afternoon paper in a joint operating agreement [with the rival *Chronicle*], so we tended to take chances and were less pressured about profits. And the tons of hate mail I got actually proved I was pushing buttons. You'd think New York would have a local political strip somewhere, in the *Voice* or something. Weird. As far as being "edgy," that merely is a reflection of San Francisco and its sensibility.

THE SAN FRANCISCO COMIC STRIP® By Don Asmussen

This Week: The Truth About Michael Bay's 'Pearl Harbor'

"Photography is truth. The cinema is truth twenty-four times per second" – Jean-Luc Godard

The Chronicle

VETERANS ON 'PEARL HARBOR' FILM: 'THERE WERE NO WOOKIES'

DIRECTOR SAYS FILM IS 'NOT A DOCUMENTARY'

Lead "Chewbacca" character said to be a composite of several real people.

The Chronicle

DIRECTOR SAYS ACTUAL PEARL HARBOR WAS BADLY PACED

'CHOPPY ATTACK LEFT VICTIMS BORED IN SPOTS'

Michael Bay is stunned to hear Roosevelt got no "back end" on the original attack.

The Chronicle

VETERANS OFFENDED BY 'PEARL HARBOR 2: PORKY'S REVENGE'

DIRECTOR SAYS SEQUEL IS 'NOT A DOCUMENTARY'

Bay claims tawdry "girls shower" plot is truthful in spirit to the original attack.

READERS, WHO DO YOU WANNA SEE TRASHED? SEND REQUESTS TO ASMUSSEND@AOL.COM

Also, I can't stand one-panel political cartooning (except for Toles). I just stare at them and their "prejudice is bad" concepts and their labels, etc., and vomit.

I like my strips to make a point, and then unmake the very same point. I don't have a clue what's really right and wrong; why pretend? As far as the "local strips" versus "*Time* magazine strips": different animals. Local strips are more controversial but seen by fewer people, and the *Time* ones are less vicious but seen by tons of people. Kinda evens out.

You have a thing about fake newspaper headlines. So does *The Onion*, but jeez. How did your obsession begin and why do you use this cartooning format so frequently?

I was a huge fan of the old *Harvard Lampoon/National Lampoon* "Not The New York Times, Not the etc..."-type par-

odies of media when I was in college, which I assume the *Onion* guys must've loved, too. Eric Idle also used to publish Monty Python books that contained lots of jokes about the very act of publishing books (which I think were an influence for Dave Eggers' "*McSweeney's*" quarterly publications).

I would do a fake news page for my college newspaper as a result. I've always been more interested in the coverage of news than the news itself (my biggest weakness as a satirist), and a lot of my earlier "San Francisco Comic Strips", though they contained no headline parodies, always made fun of news coverage itself (which Mark Alan Stamaty ['80s alternative political cartoonist who did "Washingtoon"] is a genius at).

But those earlier strips were wordy, and a reader really had to commit to my strip to get through it. It wasn't "Garfield." As I went on through the

> "Local strips are more controversial but seen by few people, and the 'Time' ones are less vicious but seen by tons of people. Kinda evens out."

years, I tried to make it less dense. Eventually this led to the current four-"newspaper"-panel format (harking back to my "Not The New York Times" obsession), which is quick to read but still gets my ideas across. I did it to make my strip quicker to read; that's it. Before, only people who were really into reading comic strips bothered to read me. I hope now that non-comics types might read me 'cause it's a quickie. Man, I look at the early ones now and can't believe people could get through them within an hour.

Because I like you, here comes another Dumbest Cartoon Interview Question Ever: Did you doodle the teachers when you were a kid?

Yeah. But I was still doing it in college.

Back to San Francisco. What's closer to the truth: a blend of '60's hangover culture and shattered dot-coms, or my view of the place as a constipated urban sprawl that can't admit it's just another American city?

Wow, you are so full of hate. I agree with the latter.

Many cities have odd mayors—I'm a New Yorker, after all—but only San Francisco had a former police chief who showered in the nude with a talk radio personality. What is it about San Francisco that spawns such bizarre personalities?

I think the city's drug haze of the '60's was so over the top that it actually genetically altered future generations. Even those who move here from elsewhere are affected. No wait, the whole country is insane. We voted in Bush. What are you talking about?

San Francisco was really a one-industry town. Now that the Web has crashed, what's next?

Plastics!

If you talk to residents of other places about San Francisco, the one thing that keeps coming up is talk of aggressive panhandlers. Why are there so many homeless people there and why are so many of them so deranged?

Well, of course, the city's reputation of charity draws them here. And remem-

Don Asmussen

ber, you can be upper-middle class and be homeless here. The prices are insane. I am currently homeless and very passive-aggressive.

During World War II, towering personalities like Churchill and Stalin changed history. Will we ever see their like again?

Garth Brooks is as close as we've gotten. But then he did that New Wave album and divided his ranks.

If you had to choose between a huge loft in an urban slum and a tiny house with a nice lawn and garden, which would you pick?

Can I have an urban slum with a nice lawn and garden?

Do you ever litter? Throwing cigarette butts on the ground counts.

I hit a softball into a lake once. That must be littering, but it was competitive littering. And I won, which is all that matters in this world.

Every day millions of cats and dogs are

An Asmussen illustration in a decidedly non-cartoony style.

The Chronicle

HP SUDDENLY DUMPS COMPAQ FOR ELLEN DEGENERES

MERGER UNRAVELS AS HP REALIZES IT'S GAY

Cynical competitors think HP is straight and only dating Ellen to generate publicity.

The Chronicle

SYBIL TO LAY OFF 25% OF MULTIPLE PERSONALITIES

FAMED PATIENT BLAMES ECONOMIC DOWNTURN

A spokesman says the cuts were needed to reposition Sybil as competitive in '02.

The Chronicle

MR. ROGERS' 'KING FRIDAY' FACES TOUGH JOB MARKET

DEAD DOT-COMS FLOOD JOB ARENA WITH KINGS

The desperate sock puppet is considering a court jester position at Kinko's.

The Chronicle

CHRISTIAN RIGHT NOW CALLING FOR BAN ON XEROXING

COPY BOYS SHOULD NOT BE 'PLAYING GOD'

Does a copy have the same rights as the document it was Xeroxed from?

The Chronicle

ARCHAEOLOGISTS NOW THINK STROM THURMOND'S NOSE WAS LOWER

POPULAR 'JURASSIC PARK' DEPICTION DISMISSED

Ohio researchers caution that it's all hypothetical due to Thurmond's erosion.

The Chronicle

ACTRESS HIRED TO REPLACE CHANDRA LEVY'S MOM ON CNN

CNN'S RAIDING OF 'NYPD BLUE' CONTINUES

If ratings continue to decline, CNN has threatened to replace its audience with actors.

The Chronicle

ASHCROFT: 'MOVIES CAUSE SCHOOL VIOLENCE'

DEMANDS BACKGROUND CHECKS AT VIDEO STORES

Critics warn that stricter movie laws would leave videos only in the hands of criminals.

The Chronicle

TOT BRINGS SAWED-OFF VIDEOCASSETTE TO SCHOOL

FOUND DAD'S PECKINPAH IN BEDROOM DRAWER

Tragedy was averted as tot is unable to get the school VCR to play the halved cassette.

The Chronicle

STOCKPILE OF 'ERNEST' MOVIES FOUND IN TOT'S HOME

COPS FOUND 'ENOUGH FOR A FILM FESTIVAL'

Parents complain that guns irresponsibly glorify the use of movies.

The Chronicle

PLAGIARISM FOUND IN BIBLE, GOD ADMITS 'CARELESSNESS'

ADMITS 'KICK IT UP A NOTCH' TAKEN FROM EMERIL BOOK

The embarrassed deity promises future printings will have the proper footnotes.

The Chronicle

'A BEAUTIFUL MIND' FILM SUGGESTS JOHN NASH'S LIFE IS ONLY 2 HOURS LONG

ACTUAL LIFE WAS 73 YRS, 364 DAYS & 22 HOURS LONGER

Historians also say that swelling music and montage were never used in Nash's actual life.

The Chronicle

COOKED BOOKS ONLY 'INSPIRED BY' REAL EVENTS, CLAIMS ENRON

PROFITS WERE CHANGED FOR 'DRAMATIC PURPOSES'

Enron defends its accounting methods as a stab at a "bigger truth."

---

killed in animal shelters. Now that I've told you this, are you going to adopt a cat or dog? Why not?

No. I already have three cats. I do wish Garfield would be killed.

What kinds of compromises do you make to do work for *Time* magazine? Have you ever compromised your editorial integrity?

No, 'cause I have very little. Like I said before, I don't have a firm grasp of right and wrong (I blame that on television), so I don't experience compromise. My only complaint would be that *Time* doesn't let me make fun of Wolf Blitzer 'cause AOL-Time Warner is part of CNN. Every week I send in a sketch making fun of Blitzer and every week they pretend their fax machine didn't work. I was just thinking, maybe Wolf Blitzer would be a good answer for that towering personality/Stalin question you asked...

Which is your favorite war?

I thought "The Empire Strikes Back" was the best one, 'cause it was darker than the first one. Irvin Kirschner directed World War II, right?

Your cartoons are created by an artist with a remarkably sharp knowledge and understanding of American pop culture. Is that necessary to do good political cartoons? Could a foreigner ever get to know Americana the way you do?

Yakov Smirnoff thrived. I think pop culture knowledge is overrated. It merely allows me to compare a politician to Scott Baio instead of some other figure from the history of politics that might be more appropriate. All I have to do is mention Milli Vanilli and I don't have to know anything about history or satire to get a laugh (see Yakov Smirnoff at top of this answer for example).

Ben Affleck and Keanu Reeves: Who's the better actor?

I like Casey Affleck. Is there a Casey Reeves? I bet he's good!

What's the future of the American newspaper? Will alternative weeklies ever surpass them in terms of readership and/or profitability?

Not if New Times [a Phoenix-based alternative weekly chain known for stamping its boilerplate designs on its new acquisitions] keeps buying them all. They just redesigned Oakland's *East Bay Express* so it looks just like *SF Weekly* or any other New Times pub. The weeklies are looking more and more like the dailies. All the same, wherever you are in the country. This seems a shame for so-called "alternatives." But it's important to keep accumulating profits.

Do you drive? If so, please describe the worst case of road rage you've ever experienced or been responsible for.

In San Francisco I use Muni (the bus system). It is so annoying and badly-run that all passengers are angry all the time. Incidents of road sanity are actually rarer. That is more shocking. We report when someone doesn't shoot someone.

Are you a registered voter? Do you vote in every election?

Yes. Unlike Ben Affleck, I am registered and have voted in all the elections I have been allowed to vote in. I assume Casey Affleck has done the same. He seems more responsible than Ben, and more talented.

Generally, are fruits or vegetables the more satisfying gastronomic experience?

I love Hamburger Helper, the Chili Mac flavor, which is hard to find nowadays. Is that a fruit or vegetable?

What is the single most important thing you would like people to remember about you? About your work?

I want them to remember that I voted more than Ben Affleck. My work will be forgotten.

Tom Tomorrow

His "This Modern World" sets the standard by which other alternative weekly comics are judged

If you read an alternative weekly newspaper, odds are that it carries the work of Tom Tomorrow. Beginning in the late '80's, "This Modern World's" retro drawing style and potent mix of straightforward anger and sarcastic humor has earned several prizes, including a Robert F. Kennedy Journalism Award. "This Modern World" appears in numerous weeklies, including *The Village Voice, San Francisco Bay Guardian* and *New Times Los Angeles.* It also runs on a freelance basis in such prestigious venues as *The New York Times, The New Yorker* and *The American Prospect.* His cartoons appear in collections published by St. Martin's Press. Now 40, Tomorrow has lost none of the vitriol or energy that fuels his strip, and will likely continue to be a potent political cartoonist for years to come.

TED RALL: "This Modern World" appears in about 100 newspapers, mostly alternative weeklies. To what do you attribute your strip's success?

TOM TOMORROW: Closer to 150. I wouldn't presume to try to explain why. I just fall to my knees every evening and thank whatever deities may exist that I don't have to get on the subway and go to some office job.

Your cartoons began as an '80's anti-consumerist postpunk exploration in the

Tom Tomorrow at the 2000 Democratic National Convention.

now-defunct San Francisco magazine *Processed World.* "This Modern World" differs noticeably from its early incarnation, with the notable exception of its continued reliance on "found" art and '50's clip-art style. What changes did you make consciously and otherwise, and why?

I don't know if I can answer this question. It hasn't been such a conscious effort. You do something for a long time, you tend to develop some level of competency. At this point, I'm not good at much—God help me if I ever have to get a real job—but I'm very good at being Tom Tomorrow.

For many years, editors and readers would confuse your work and mine. Does that still happen to you? Why do you think it happened in the first place, given how different our stuff looks and reads?

It is because we were both the angry new kids on

the block, both with a left-liberal sensibility and styles which—while completely dissimilar—were alike in that they both resembled nothing else in political cartooning. It doesn't seem to happen so much anymore, possibly because we've both been around a long time, and people are hopefully more familiar with our distinct styles. You know, my cartoon's the one with the penguin, yours is the one where somebody always gets shot at the end.

When did you first learn that life was fundamentally unfair?

I am not sure I ever believed otherwise.

Could one of your cartoons ever improve the world in the slightest? Has that ever happened?

It seems unlikely. You have to want to save the world in order to get up every day and do this work, but in order to maintain your sanity, you simultaneously have to understand that you're just not going to. On the other hand, I do get a lot of mail from peo-

ple in their late teens who have grown up with my work, writing to let me know that I have helped to shape their view of the world. I guess that's the best you can hope for.

A few years ago you began incorporating imagery from your digital camera within your work. Do you consider it an important part of your work to use the latest available technology? After all, you always seem to have some new gadget whenever I meet you.

The technology is just a tool. For a long time, I didn't use anything more technologically advanced than a photocopier. My present computer is several generations old at this point, and, I am told, hopelessly outdated—but it serves my needs perfectly well at this time.

I'll cop to a bit of a gadget fetish, but I'm not a gearhead. I don't care how the stuff works, I don't care what's under the hood—I'm only interested in what I can do with it. Using these tools has allowed me to expand and experiment—the digital camera was particularly integral to the work I did last year at the political conventions—but they're just tools.

You got married recently. Do you plan to have kids? If so, are you worried that your dysfunctional childhood will make you a less-than-perfect father?

I didn't have an Ozzie-and-Harriet childhood, it's true—there were multiple divorces and numerous moves to different states and the usual tug of war between the parents—and it left scars, of course, but whose childhood doesn't? I guess the important thing, as fucked up as the situation was sometimes, is that I never doubted that I was wanted or loved. I don't suppose anyone is a perfect father, but you do the best you can. My wife and I are a good team, I figure we'll do okay.

I read something once that stuck with me, in which a writer compared raising his children to shouting at characters on a movie screen—when the hero avoids danger, you think you've helped out; when he falls into the villain's trap, you've failed him. I suspect that's a lot of what parenthood is like—ultimately out of control. You do what you can—try to provide a happy and stable home, put in your time, and hope for the best.

You're a fairly reticent guy in person, but you become this amazing showman

when you do book signings and other public appearances. What are you tapping into with your public persona?

As a civilian I don't really care if I'm the center of attention or not, but when you're speaking in public, you *are* the center of attention—people have come specifically to see you because they enjoy your work, and that's an extraor-

dinary thing. People have busy lives, they have jobs, children, they're tired at the end of the day. If they take the time to come to one of my events, I want them to feel that it was not a wasted evening. So I try to make it interesting—with slides and sometimes videos. In New York last year, we even had an interactive Sparky on a video screen (being controlled by my animation partner behind the scenes), who actually answered questions from the audience. And there's an energy you tap into, especially at a good event, when it's been well publicized and you've got a crowd and the thing just builds on itself. It doesn't always click, but on a good night it's magical.

You're in virtually every major alternative weekly in the nation. Do you worry that at some point editors will tire of your work—as some say they have with Matt Groening's "Life in Hell" and Lynda Barry's Ernie Pook's Comeek" before us? If that happened, what would you do next?

Sure, most likely my career will have an arc like anyone else's. And of course I worry about it in much the same way that I might worry about developing a brain tumor or losing my home in a fire. But there's not much you can do about it except to keep plugging away and trying to keep your work fresh. If you want to keep people's interest, you have to avoid the ruts which you see writers and cartoonists fall into sometimes (is [*New York Times* columnist] Maureen Dowd capable of writing a column without a banal pop culture reference?).

But if it all goes to hell some day and all my papers drop me at the same time, well, I had a good run—I haven't had a real job in something like 12 years at this point. I'll find something else to do. If I worried too much about this sort of thing I probably never would have become a cartoonist to begin with—it's not exactly the sort of gig that comes with a lot of guarantees. Although, really, we probably have more job security than you might think—I mean, people get laid off all the time. If you're syndicated, there's no single person who can call you on the phone and tell you that you no longer have a job. No one individual has that power over you.

Your depictions of politicians: Do you run them through your computer and abstract them, are they drawn, or a mixture of both?

They are digitally-redrawn images working from source material. I suspect it looks easier than it is—you still have to have an eye, to understand which details define a person's face, and more importantly, character. That dull look in Bush's eyes, for instance, or the aura of evil which emanates from Dick Cheney. The computer allows me

The cartoonist as rock star: Tom, center, works a 2000 Ralph Nader rally.

to shift lines a fraction one way or another, to add or subtract wrinkles, and to just keep tinkering with it until I've got what I'm after.

Will cartoonists ever make a significant portion of their livings from the Internet?

I don't have the slightest idea. Not in the near future, certainly, but probably someday. Depends on how it all eventually shakes out. We're still in the earliest stages of this thing. Ten years ago, nobody had an e-mail address. When I started putting my work up online in 1993, people thought it was some sort of revolutionary act. The net is at the stage television was at in maybe 1940. They knew something was going to happen, but they didn't know it was going to be "Survivor" and "Blind Date."

Do you still listen to punk rock, and if so, to whom? Does music play a role in your work or your politics?

I was renting a studio apartment uptown as a workspace for awhile, and the guy I shared a wall with was a stoner jazz musician, who thought nothing of having all-day jam sessions complete with electric bass and incessantly pounding drums. I tried talking with him and explaining that I was having trouble concentrating on my little cartoons, but there was no meeting in the middle, no compromise, and it was really driving me nuts, so every time they'd start up I'd turn my speakers against the wall and blast old Dead Kennedys tapes at full volume. But mostly, I spend my days listening to news and talk radio.

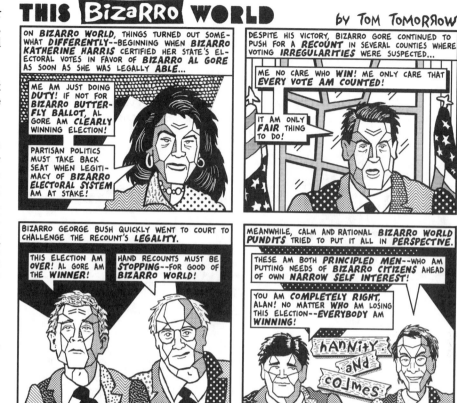

During the 2000 presidential campaign, you gave speeches at rallies for Green Party candidate, Ralph Nader. I think you also did some cartoons for them, and you overtly supported him in your work. Did you receive criticism for crossing the line between objective journalism and electioneering?

Any political cartoonist who imagines himself to be an objective journalist should be in another line of work. The whole point of this job is to express your opinions. I have always been an advocate for one thing or another, and when

Nader came along and looked like he was making a serious run, a serious attempt to get these issues out into the mainstream, and they asked me if I'd lend my name to the campaign, it seemed like it was time to either put up or shut up.

Yes, of course I received criticism, especially from whining Democrats who blame Nader for the fact that their pathetic candidate lost the election by 150 votes or whatever it was, but you know—getting a few nasty e-mails is not exactly the highest price anyone has ever paid for speaking their mind.

"Bloom County" had Opus. Pat Oliphant's editorial cartoons have that little penguin guy in the corner. Now you have Sparky the Wonder Penguin (though sometimes he claims to be an auk). Did he start out as a satire of cartoon penguinism? If so, why isn't he dead yet? And if he's an auk, shouldn't you have told us that when you first brought him into the world?

Wilbur the Talking Stomach died a few years back. Hasn't there been enough tragedy, Ted? Enough suffering? What will it take to satisfy this bloodlust of yours? Anyway, I've got big marketing plans ahead. Forget Tickle-Me-Elmo, the Rant-and-Rave Sparky is going to make me *millions*. Not to mention the Sparkyland theme park and entertainment complex.

You've often been accused of being a shill for Bill Clinton and/or the Democratic Party, yet you've often taken positions critical of both. Why do you think you attract that sort of criticism? And do your leftie fans get angry when you take liberal sacred cows to task?

The weird thing about that is that my work is all a matter of public record; anyone who considers me a shill for Clinton or the Democrats is more than welcome to sift through my online archive, which goes back more than ten years, and try to find a shred of evidence to support the charge. I couldn't be more upfront in my dislike for both bought-and-paid-for major parties, and yet whenever I focus specifically on one, I am accused of shilling for the other.

It's this binary, either/or political philosophy—if you ain't fer us, you're agin' us. It's impossibly simpleminded. And of course, the people who accuse me of being a partisan hack are usually themselves partisan hacks. As for the liberals in my audience, yes, they were pretty annoyed with me during the last election, and continue to be annoyed with me when I point out that much of what Bush has done so far, from arsenic levels to the Kyoto Protocol to Alaskan oil drilling, has often been nothing more than a continuation of Clinton Administration policies, albeit without the decorative sprinkling of liberal pieties. This is a simple statement of fact, this isn't debatable—but liberals don't want to hear it. They want a simple world in which the Republicans are bad and the Democrats are good, and I just don't see the world that way—and after eight years of the Clinton White House, I really don't understand how anyone can still see the world that way, unless they also believe in Santa Claus and the Tooth Fairy.

Ever been on "Politically Incorrect"? Would you want to be? What's the worst/stupidest media appearance of your career?

I've done other TV stuff, but not PI. If they asked me I'm sure I'd accept, if only for the exposure. I don't know if you've done the show, but frankly, they could use people like us. It's not a political roundtable, it's an entertainment show

Tomorrow with covert political ally Ollie North.

posing as a political roundtable.

Bill Maher seems like a smart guy, but I doubt if half his guests could name the Secretary of State if you held a gun to their heads. A friend of mine in Los Angeles was told by the show's producer that they don't like to book liberal political commentators because they believe most of the actors they have on their show are liberals, so what you get is conservative commentators who are capable of cogent, if misguided, arguments squaring off against some actor who might have read a newspaper at some point in the last month or two, maybe.

I did a cartoon about PI once that ran in *TV Guide* (most likely ensuring that I will never in fact be invited on the show) in which the roundtable consisted of "an empty-headed actor, a blond

pundit, a burned-out rocker and the dog from the Taco Bell ads." The dog was the only one who had anything intelligent to say.

Worst media experience? Johnny Rotten's internet radio show, without a doubt. He'd throw out some moronic question like, "Republicans are really bad, aren't they?" and I'd have to come up with something intelligent to say in response. There were no commercial breaks, and I ended up carrying most of the show, riffing desperately, trying to run the clock out. Longest hour of my life that didn't involve dental surgery.

Yo, your cartoons—so many words! Why can't you keep it simple?

If the world were a simpler place, my cartoons would reflect that.

Clay Butler

"Sidewalk Bubblegum" uses single-panel gag cartoons that actually matter

Santa Cruz-based, Illinois-born Clay Butler's "Sidewalk Bubblegum" explores the territory between sight gags and politically-charged rage each week in the *Santa Cruz Sentinel*, *Funny Times*, *Comic Relief* and Finland's *Hufvudstadsbladet*. Butler, 36, is a self-described "vegetarian, atheist, socialist, anarchist, surfer and partner of a bisexual woman in a committed 13-year non-monogamous relationship."

TED RALL: Many of your cartoons have a distinct California flavor—political activists, New Age, the environment, etc. Even your cartoon characters sport that tell-tale T-shirt and chinos look. How do your surroundings influence and inspire you? Would your work change if you moved somewhere distinctly different, say, London?

CLAY BUTLER: Most definitely. It's important to me that my work not only reflect intellectual and philosophical realities but also reflect cultural realities. Hair styles, slang, regionalisms, clothes and buildings are all integral to carrying the message. If you fail to reflect the truths, it tends to dis-tract from your point or even discredit it entirely. After all, how can I critique our dependency on oil if I can't even draw a gas pump properly, or how can I illustrate the horrors of war if my dead bodies look like mannequins and my soldiers talk like poli-sci majors! I'm really anal about these things. Even cartoon characters need to reflect kinetic realities of human movement if you are to fully empathize with their situation. You need to see yourself in the characters' eyes. It's hard for me to describe how important it is that my strip looks beautiful. I still get excited about a perfectly drawn hand! As for moving to London, it wouldn't be that hard to include Bobbies and crooked teeth.

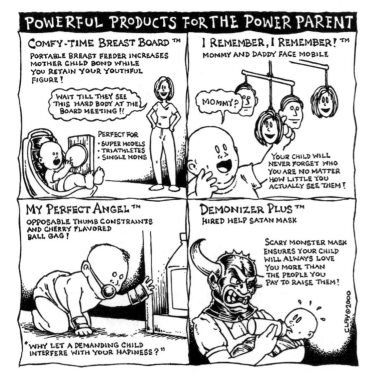

Speaking of California, your early work often deals with the so-called War on Drugs and you call (not so subtly) for legalization. Nowadays, you rarely delve into the subject. Have you gone clean and sober? Were you a stoner? Inquiring minds, and the NSA, wanna know.

Actually, I'm straight. Never smoked, drank, did drugs, ever. Most people find that strange; after all, wasn't I curious? I suppose I was as curious about drugs and alcohol as I was to finding out if poo really tasted as bad as it smelled. Really, I never gave it a second thought. As for legalization, I'm in the uncomfortable position of being opposed to the use of drugs and alcohol and yet unwavering in my support of a person's right to alter their consciousness and body in any way they see fit. It's my commitment to human rights that creates these paradoxes. Damn these humanist values! Damn them to hell!

Again with the drug thing, I'm intrigued. I would never have believed the pot-as-a-gateway-drug theory if I hadn't seen it operate firsthand among friends. Don't you believe that, for many users, they inevitably start wanting and needing something with a little more oomph than pot? And if so, isn't it the government's role to protect people from themselves?

I suppose it's a gateway in the most pedestrian sense but then again human development is all about gateways. Crawling is a gateway to walking, listening to music is a gateway to becoming a musician and interaction with other people is a gateway to insights on human nature.

Does it bother me to see people destroying themselves with drugs and alcohol? You bet. Does the government have a responsibility to stop them? I suppose that depends on if you believe people have a right of self-determination, to control their own bodies and thoughts. From a humanist perspective, it's the government's job to protect people from each other, not from themselves. The government's role is to act as a referee of sorts, to find some kind of balance between an individual's right to control their own life and another person's right to not be exploited or hurt.

Are you religious? Do you believe in a God?

No and no. I have no interest entertaining fantasies of an afterlife, of supreme beings, souls, spirits, ghosts, astrology, palm reading, numerology, crystals, free trade, trickle-down economics, privatization, etc. If we were living in a society that valued intelligence, free inquiry, logic and reason, most people would snicker at such a silly question. Let's face it, there's more direct evidence for the existence of the Tooth Fairy then there is for God. Almost everyone has had the real-life experience of placing a tooth under a pillow and then finding a quarter in its place in the morning. How can we ignore such overwhelming proof?! Christians wish they had that kind of hard evidence for their case!

War is a favorite topic of yours, yet the United States hasn't fought a "real" war since Vietnam—just a bunch of low-rent skirmishes in Afghanistan, Panama, Iraq, and Grenada. Are you worried about the prospect of another "real" war or are your critiques focused on these micro-mini-wars? And is there ever such a thing as a good war?

The idea of another "real" war is not a concern of mine. It's obvious that the capitalist class would never allow it as it would be incredibly disruptive to the global flow of goods and services. Chaos hurts business; stability nurtures it! It's that simple. Micro-mini wars on the other hand can still serve a useful purpose for the ruling class and can even expand markets and profits. But even this is starting to die out as the ruling class discovers that they can accomplish the same ends with far subtler and less expensive means, NAFTA and GATT being the most obvious examples. As

with all wars, it benefits the few and devastates the many.

Nina Paley, a leftie cartoonist who used to draw "Nina's Adventures," mocked "soft liberals" — squishy Democrat types holding up protest signs at demonstrations. Are such people wasting their time? If you could snap your fingers, would you will a revolution and if so, what kind?

I wouldn't say that they're wasting their time. Every little bit helps. It's the lack of systemic critique and their infatuation with trendy causes that turn my stomach.

The Mumia Abu-Jamal case is a prime example. To make him the poster boy for racism and oppression is strategically foolish because one, he's accused of killing a white police officer, and two, his imprisonment is not as clear-cut an example as both sides make a compelling argument for. There are many other people on death row who actually have hard DNA evidence of their innocence but the liberals aren't interested because they're not attractive, they're not articulate, their alleged victim has no symbolic value, or they have no published tomes of treasured poetry and essays. If Mumia were illiterate or ugly, or had just been accused of killing some street punk, there would be no movement. Period.

As for revolution, I think it's a poor choice for change. Revolutions tend to attract reactionaries that have the same infatuation with power and control as the people they claim to want to overthrow. It's best to change things with slow, organized and methodical means that build a foundation as they move forward.

SNCC [the Student Nonviolent Coordinating Committee] in the '60's was a fine example. Look at the stability and quality of the people they attracted to their movement, as opposed to the screwballs that were attracted to the much sexier and flashy Black Panther Party.

Please describe the worst experience of your life.

I suppose being gay-bashed in Denver, Colorado, is pretty close to the top of the list. It was at night and I was going to art school at the time. A couple of guys accosted me and basically said they're going to kill me because I'm a faggot. Fortunately, I was with a friend of mine who was pretty big and had a more traditionally male demeanor and appearance. He was able to calm them down, so it never progressed past hard shoving and threats. These guys were seriously intoxicated and were part of a much larger group by the corner. If I had been alone, I'm not sure if I would be alive today.

Up until that moment I felt completely at ease walking around at night. After all, I was an adult and no longer in high school so I felt bullies were no longer a problem. Apparently, I was wrong. I still feel anxiety whenever I'm in a big city at night; I just can't get past the feeling that I'm going to be murdered at any moment.

Do you hold any stances that would traditionally be considered right of center? I'm thinking specifically of a cartoon you did about "power parents" who warehouse their kids in daycare centers. That could illustrate a Dr. Laura Schlessinger book. Do progressives get pissed at you for deviating from the party line?

People who I would call "progressives" as opposed to "liberal" tend to love the cartoons that deviate. Which I think hits at the central philosophical motivation for progressives, which is progress in social, political and economic justice. To do this effectively, you need to be on your toes, flexible and open-minded as well as possess a universal commitment to justice. Since my cartoons address fundamental realities, progressives love 'em.

Liberals, on the other hand, have very little interest in actual injustice and are more concerned about the perception of injustice. For example, progressives want to fight racism while liberals want to fight the perception that our society is racist. Hate-crime laws are a classic example of liberal thinking. Hate-crime laws are at best grandstanding, and at worst a serious distortion of our concepts of equal protection. How can we make killing a woman because she's black or lesbian a more serious offense than killing a woman to get her purse? The net result is still one dead woman.

To place one victim higher because of their race or sexual orientation or because of the intent and beliefs of the victimizer is truly sick. If you really believe it is a more serious crime to murder someone because of their race, then

is it a lesser crime to kill a racist? After all, we all oppose racism. Why not send a message to society that we find these people reprehensible by decriminalizing their murders altogether?

As for the cartoon you mentioned, that one has more to do with the selfish, got-to-have-it all, results-oriented parenting that places status and achievement over all other human endeavors. In the case of the cartoon, the child becomes nothing more than a symbol or an object to be manipulated to satisfy the parents' agenda. Attacking the concept of daycare itself was not my intent.

Do you like mainstream political cartoons? What works about them and what doesn't?

Besides Tom Toles and Kirk Anderson, no. It's kind of depressing, really. When I look at mainstream political cartoons, which are really editorial cartoons in a sense that they serve the purpose of repeating and reinforcing the editorial content of their paper, I see a wasteland of lost opportunity and potential. While we can assign some blame to the consolidation of our media, the cartoonists themselves who appear to believe in nothing except

doing whatever it takes to maintain their job must carry the largest blame. Just follow any mainstream political cartoonist for a month. I challenge you to find any consistent philosophical, ethical or moral thread running through their work. For the most part, they consist of cheap jokes, clichés and stereotypes that reinforce commonly-held superficial beliefs. It's disgusting.

Peter Kuper

This multitalented New Yorker applies several distinct approaches to his work

An editor and co-founder of the influential zine *World War 3 Illustrated,* cartoonist Peter Kuper also does numerous freelance illustrations for *The New York Times,* draws "Spy vs. Spy" for *Mad* magazine and produces a wordless alternative-weekly comic strip, "Eye of the Beholder," which toys with graphic and psychological perspective to make statements about humanity and society. Recognizable for his scratchboard and stencil-based illustration styles, he is the author of the critically-acclaimed books *The System* and *ComicsTrips,* and most recently a coffee-table retrospective of his career, *Speechless.* Political and sentimental, popular and populist, the multi-talented Kuper is just 43.

TED RALL: Your book *Speechless* contains a cool timeline of your life and career. I was struck by a photograph showing you looking happy and enthusiastic in the center of the front row of your first-grade class. Alan Bullock's comparative histories of Hitler and Stalin contains first-grade class pictures. Both photos show the future dictators looking glum and arrogant in the center of the last row. I don't know if this means anything, but I figured I'd start with that.

PETER KUPER: This picture was taken at the beginning of the year. By the end of

first grade, my teacher, Miss Minino, had knocked that happy, enthusiastic grin off my face, and I have been fighting to recover it ever since.

You've done political cartoons in numerous guises and formats, but your most overtly political material appears in the magazine you co-edit with Seth Tobocman, *World War 3 Illustrated.* How did you meet Seth, and how did *WW3* get started? Were you trying to compete with *Raw?*

Seth and I were in the same first-grade

class in Cleveland, Ohio and lived a street away from one another. Both our fathers taught at Case Western Reserve University and our sisters were best friends. By the seventh grade Seth and I were beginning to publish our first fanzine together since we had both found a mutual enthusiasm for comics. Our first effort was brilliantly called "Phanzine" which we published in 1970.

Then we took over a mimeo newsletter called "G.A.S Lite" (it was the official magazine of the Cleveland Graphic Arts Society, a group of local fans). We turned it into an offset zine and included interviews we got through the mail and at comic book conventions (among them R. Crumb and William Gaines [*Mad's* publisher] and a lot of superhero artists) and comics by various fan artists. Seth and I fell out in high school but both found our way to New York and rekindled the friendship. Seth was in film school at NYU and I was attending Pratt Institute. Seth dropped out of NYU, finding the whole film deal to be too complicated, and joined me at Pratt.

We both had been drawing comics, but could find no outlet for publishing them—this was in 1979, and the entire underground comix scene had collapsed (due in great part to the outlawing of "head shops"

PEANUTS 2000

which had been an important outlet for distribution). Since we already had experience publishing a zine, it was a natural leap to make the move to self-publish. We also were interested in exposing other work we admired to light, not just to create a vanity press for our own art. The first issue of *Raw* had not been published when we began *World War 3* so it wasn't any kind of influence—we did happen to share a long-arm stapler when we put our first issues together, though! We never saw it in terms of competition, just a mutual love of the form. *Raw* was also in another league with expensive printing and color, aiming for a coffee table art book quality while we were interested in a low cost newsprint that would have a cheap cover price that students like ourselves could afford.

What is the purpose/mission of *WW3 Illustrated*? It started at the dawn of the Reagan era and now continues in Bush Deux. Do you worry that the project may have played out its role?

If anything, *WW3* seems to have a more vital role to play given the present administration and there is no end to the number of new people who want to

> "I see the magazine as a microcosm of the kind of society I want to live in... one that is inclusive & open to a variety of ideas and styles and is not striving to be a private club."

make the magazine happen. When Seth and I started it, we didn't sit down and write a mission statement, we just felt compelled to create a place to publish work. The political atmosphere at that time, with a hostage crisis in Iran, people talking about nuking left and right and joke candidate Ronald Reagan actually winning support, produced a sense of urgency that got us in gear. It is also important to point out that although Seth and I started it and have been ever involved with it over the last 23 years, there have also been a number of other people that have played important roles in keeping it going, like Sabrina Jones, Scott Cunningham and Kevin Pyle to name just a few.

In many ways, I see the magazine as a microcosm of the kind of society I want to live in. It's one that is inclusive and open to a variety of ideas and styles and is not striving to be a private club. It is a hard balance to pull off since you sacrifice perfection when you allow first-timers and artists who are still developing to get a shot, but this has lead to some amazing results. Artists like Eric Drooker and James Romberger developed major work in the pages of *WW3* and, for that matter, I got to cut my teeth publishing my own comics there and

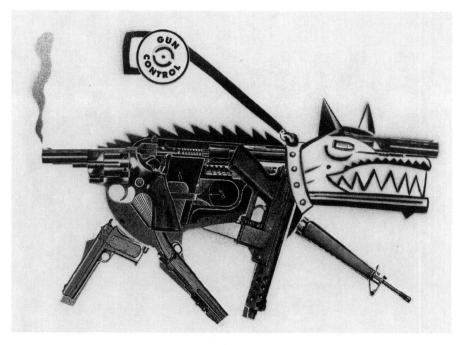

developing my politics in a group setting. Getting a magazine to work is as good a place to start as any to see if you can form a new society that can survive without imploding.

You became a father recently. (Congrats on that.) It's often said that parenthood leads to small-c conservatism, and even to the big-C version. Have you noticed that happen to you?

Every life-change alters the kinds of work I produce. When I was single, I had one perspective, married another, and with a daughter, a whole new outlook (greatly influenced by years of sleep-deprivation!). But on the contrary, I think my sense of urgency has increased. The idea that I fiddled while the world she will inherit burned is an accusation I don't want to be tried for in her teen years.

My politics are just naturally evolving as I age and gain new experience—I'm always trying to find more effective ways of communicating, and more and more I find humor is the way I want to go. The most conservative effect, if you can call it that, has been my work schedule. After years of working nights and weekends, I have turned into a working stiff who goes into his office at about the same early time, and comes home at about the same time. Surprise, surprise, I find I get a lot more accomplished on this schedule and don't have to work as much to have the same output. Of course, money is an issue that I have to contend with, having a child, but I try to not have it take over my work choices. It does, of course, but fortunately I've found that doing what is closest to my heart is my

Emily Kuper and her dad, about 1998.

best work, and, at least these days, the money usually follows.

There are still a number of projects I'd like to do that are hard since they involve little or no advance pay. These are mostly comic books, which I want to do more of, but having a child has made them harder to make the time for. I just have to be more creative with my time, work faster, clone myself and spend less time responding to interview questions.

You're Jewish, you've worked on a kibbutz. Do you believe in God? And is there a solution to the conflict between Israelis and Palestinians?

I believe in God, and ghosts, and UFOs among many other things. Particularly when I've been traveling, I do feel a force connecting things together; GOD is as good a word to describe it as any. Religion is a whole other bag, and that's where I have lots of problems. The moment someone tries to

insist on the specific shape this connection must take, I'm gone. Ritual has its place, it is good to mark events so life doesn't turn into a blur, or take time to hold hands and be thankful for the food on the table, but the outrageousness of telling anyone you know what God has planned is at best an exercise of enormous egotism and at worst as close as I want to come to Satan.

As far as Israel is concerned, I have no answer. I spent a year living there at the age of ten when my father taught there on a sabbatical. I remember the feeling of righteousness that was in the air back in 1969 following the Six Day War, and the underdog status that Israel held. But upon subsequent returns in 1978, '84 and finally in '89 this feeling drained away. Some of this had to do with my outlook going from a kid to adult understanding of the complexities, but I think much of it is in the tone that Israelis acquired. Seeing Israeli soldiers harass Arabs and a generation of people growing up with hatred has made it lose its righteous footing. Of course it's not like the

insane Arab bombers are creating sympathy either. It's a mess that will only get worse as each side escalates the "eye for an eye" approach until everyone's blind.

You got a National Endowment for the Arts grant for *World War 3 Illustrated*. But don't you think there's something a little weird about government bureaucrats deciding which artists deserve financial support and which ones don't?

There's something very weird about government bureaucrats having any say regarding any art, but considering the billions they put towards making World War 3 a real event, it's fine with me if they drop a penny on *World War 3* the magazine.

What's the conceit behind "Eye of the Beholder" and what is its target market?

It started in the *New York Times'* City section back in 1993. I was asked to try and come up with a strip that had no ongoing characters, but had some ongoing consistency. Hmmm. I realized that if there were words, each week I'd be contending with an editor adjusting my syntax and I've always found wordless comics appealing and a good synthesis between my illustrations and my comics.

I found the open-ended idea of the strip that could follow a person, place or thing (generally with a last-panel kicker showing the point of view you are following) gave me plenty of room to move around. At first I tried to have something in the last panel of each strip connect to the next strip, but it was over-thinking it.

The *Times* ran the strip for about six months before an ad replaced it, and I took

that group of strips and sent them to alt papers. I've ended up doing it since for a number of papers around the country and online.

One night at dinner you told me that you were often depressed. How come? Are many cartoonists depressive people?

I have often felt like there is a black cloud following me around making it all the more difficult to create, but I've discovered it is a very busy cloud since it has to cover all cartoonists and musicians and writers and actors and....

Being an artist and trying to do work from the heart is a short path to insanity, given the complicated number of things that go into making that work and getting it out to an audience. To be successful you have to not only create the work but promote it, and these are diametrically-opposed skills. It is also an exercise in frustration to work in an art form like comics that is still struggling simply to be recognized as such, but it depends on the day you catch me how I feel about all this. When the whole process comes together and an illustration or book project flies, there is no higher high, and I'd probably go postal if I had a 9-to-5.

Please describe one moment of perfect joy.

Watching Richard Nixon, with sweat on his upper lip, resigning on national television.

You've been arrested and are being tortured. You can choose between a week without sleep and a week without food. Which do you pick and why?

That's easy, I'll take the week with no sleep— I'm not sure how well I'd take the no food, but as a parent I've already experienced being under house arrest, being tortured by an infant's endless screaming and going for years without enough sleep, so I know that much—I can survive.

TRUTH OR DARE?

Expanded "PROFILING"

Read all about it!

Jen Sorensen

Her "Slowpoke" is more than a strip, it's a way of life

A 27-year-old native of rural Lancaster County, Pennsylvania, Jen Sorensen's senior thesis at the University of Virginia (her major was anthropology) was on bawdy humor in under-ground comics drawn by women. She is now beginning to garner attention for exactly that genre of humor—with more than a dash of thoughtful political commentary tossed in for good measure—with her strip "Slowpoke." "Slowpoke" appears in the humor monthly *Funny Times, Punchline Urban Manifest* in Richmond, Virginia, Charlottesville's *C-Ville Weekly* and other alternative papers. Sorensen maintains a day job doing web design at her alma mater to keep her in art supplies and used CDs.

A young Jen Sorensen and The Hulk at Christmas.

TED RALL: You've cited Disney as an early artistic influence. But many of your peers consider Walt and Mickey and the gang to be the incarnation of pure evil, representing a sordid '50s Americana created by hopelessly exploited cartoonists and animators. Is the influence ironic or straight-up?

JEN SORENSEN: What I found profoundly influential was the art and writing of Carl Barks (and later, Don Rosa) who created these extremely sophisticated Uncle Scrooge and Donald Duck stories with all sorts of witty side gags and pop culture references. The only "Disneyesque" aspect of these stories, as far as I was concerned, was the cast of characters. As a kid I collected the Barks reprints published by Whitman and then Gladstone. Inspired by these stories, I would then draw my own comics, typically adventure narratives with lots of spies. Barks often populated his tales with sinister, vaguely European spies, a theme which reflected the James Bond heyday of the '60s. Other influences on my art include Basil Wolverton, R. Crumb, and Mad magazine.

To clarify, I actually hate most everything Disney has ever produced, in particular their animation. Even as a kid I had zero interest in Disney movies. The Disney "style" has always struck me as utterly soulless, generic, and alienating. Every film seems to have this cloying grandeur about it, which I call the "prefab classic" syndrome —that is, when a movie contrives to be a timeless classic by virtue of its sheer lushness. Yawn!

Women editorial cartoonists—especially in the world of underground comics—are "supposed" to tackle such subjects as their periods, abortion, hateful men, etc. Yet those topics don't crop up much in "Slowpoke." Why not?

You know, I just find many of these subjects to be horrible clichés. With the exception of abortion, which is an issue I take seriously though I haven't done a cartoon about it yet, things like periods and hateful men have been covered to death. Moreover, these subjects don't play a very large role in my life. There are "masculine" cartoon clichés that I find equally boring, like gratuitous shock-value humor. I'm much more interested in politics and broader cultural phenomena, and humor for humor's sake.

What is your mission as a cartoonist? Is it your job to make readers laugh, think, or both?

THE SAD TALE OF **UGLIÁN**

ONE DAY SOME FISHERMEN DISCOVERED LITTLE UGLIÁN FLOATING IN THE OCEAN OFF THE FLORIDA COAST.

LOOK! WE CAUGHT A KID!

S.S. SEACOW

JEEZ, HE'S UGLY! THROW HIM BACK!

UGLIÁN EVENTUALLY SWAM ASHORE AND SOUGHT OUT HIS RELATIVES IN MIAMI.

GRANDMA! GRANDPA! IT IS ME, UGLIÁN!

GOOD LORD!

RUN, DEAR, RUN!

UGLIÁN WOUND UP IN THE CUSTODY OF U.S. OFFICIALS, WHOSE PLANS TO RETURN HIM TO HIS HOMELAND WERE MET WITH RESISTANCE.

NO CHILD THIS UGLY COULD HAVE COME FROM MY COUNTRY!

WE WILL NOT ACCEPT HIM!

HOWEVER, BEFORE AN INTERNATIONAL INCIDENT COULD DEVELOP, EVERYONE LOST INTEREST.

HEY, I WONDER WHATEVER HAPPENED TO THAT UGLIÁN KID...

WHO?

My goal with "Slowpoke" is to present a solidly-written piece of humor that usually entails some form of social or political commentary exposing distinctly ludicrous aspects of American life. Some of my cartoons are more overtly political than others, but I usually strive to make a point, even if it is a casual cultural observation. Cartoons are a great medium for demonstrating just how absurd something is, without ever having to say it directly.

Female cartoonists like Carol Lay and Nina Paley complain that they find their work ghettoized into "women's issues" and compilations devoted to women's comics. You debuted in something called "Action Girl," a compilation of female cartoonists. Do women cartoonists get branded as separate and less than equal, or are the complaints overstating the case?

I'm afraid my career is still too young at this point for me to clearly observe a pattern. I have participated in a few compilations concerned with women's issues, illustrating a story in "Dignifying Science" by Jim Ottaviani, for example, which features the biographies of several women scientists. But I've also had illustration work appear in DC Comics' Big Book of the '70s (I got assigned the "'70s Sexplosion!" story, partly because of Drooly Julie, and partly because the editor knew I wouldn't draw photorealistic anatomy), and my work has always been welcome in such anthologies as the Small Press EXPO annual. It's entirely plausible to me that female artists have had a tougher time of it than their male counterparts, but I haven't been in the business long enough to have any personal experiences to that effect.

Most guy cartoonists got their asses kicked by bullies in junior high school. How about you?

I had the usual cartoonist problem of finding a niche for myself and "fitting in," but I can't recall ever being physically threatened. I do remember that in second grade, I kicked a guy in the crotch at recess for some reason. I have no idea what he did to me; I'm usually loath to resort to any form of violence. I remember feeling guilty about that incident for a long time afterwards.

What, in your opinion, causes school shootings such as the one at Columbine

High School in Colorado?

First, and most obviously, the availability of guns and the carelessness of parents who own them are huge problems. Handguns should be illegal, plain and simple.

Perhaps less obvious than the problem of gun accessibility is the instant cult of celebrity that surrounds a school shooter. In America, celebrity is the highest status a person can achieve. The news media, including very respectable publications, feed into the mythology by printing actual pictures of the killers on the front pages of papers. Worse yet, the kid's face appears all over television, which as we all know is more real than real life. Not only does the kid gain notoriety and a sense of empowerment, but suddenly the act of shooting up a high school becomes a realistic possibility for others.

The result is more than just a problem of copycat killings. Bringing a gun to school gets defined as something that is done and even glorified. It's no longer a random act of violence.

So, guns kill people? What about the bullying that provokes such sprees?

Well, as my main squeeze says, "Guns don't kill people—people with guns kill people." I know bullies can be an absolute nightmare, and they certainly can provoke the rage that leads to shootings. However loathsome bullies may be, though, blowing them away is not cool. The only way to remove this temptation is to make guns inaccessible to kids, and to stop lavishing so much attention on those who do go on shooting sprees. Put the story on page two of the paper, without using the killer's name or picture. I don't need to know what they look like.

Does it really matter whether Democrats or Republicans are in charge?

Anyone who thinks there's no difference between Democrats and Republicans is a dingdong. Lots of people generalize that they're the same because they both pander to corporate interests. It's true: we live in a plutocracy condoned by a totally ignorant public. But that's a problem with the system far bigger than the people who have to operate within it, and the only way it's going to change is through massive campaign finance reform. Television ads need to be free,

and campaign funds should come from the public sector only. That said, these reforms are more likely to come about via the Democrats (along with quirky Republicans like McCain). I'm not saying Democrats are perfect, but I think there are a lot of good, well-meaning people trapped in the system.

Every day now I open up the newspaper, and Bush is committing some new atrocity that makes me sick. In spite of Gore's flaws, we almost had a president who wanted to eliminate the internal combustion engine. There is a substantial difference.

Been in any really bad car wrecks? Ever been arrested? Inquiring readers wanna know!

I was in one fairly dramatic car wreck. Not long after graduating college, I was driving my mother's Ford Taurus through a neighborhood back home in Pennsylvania. I was pulling out onto a street from a side road. I looked both ways, then started leisurely pulling out when a pickup truck going, like, 60 miles an hour appeared on my left. I tried to scoot across the street, but the truck didn't slow down and it nailed the back of my mother's car, spinning me around 180 degrees until the car came to a rest against a telephone pole. The Taurus was totaled but I was unharmed. The police ruled that no one was at fault. I hate cars; driving is a game of Russian roulette.

I haven't been arrested.

Should the United States, Mexico and Canada become one country? Has the era of the nation-state come to an end?

Oh jeez, I dunno. I think having the U.S. annexed by Canada would be a good thing. It would solve the health insurance crisis. As someone who has to pay for health insurance out-of-pocket, I find Canada pretty appealing these days.

Your recurring character Drooly Julie is a perpetually, laughable horny chick. Why'd you come up with her? Was she inspired by any women you know?

I've always gotten a kick out of R. Crumb's drawings of himself desperately humping the leg of some large and indifferent woman. I don't have a huge problem with objectification per se, so long as it goes both ways. But it historically hasn't gone both ways and that's a shame. That's why Drooly Julie was born.

It's about time someone celebrated the male form other than gay men. As far as being inspired by anyone in particular, well...let's just say Drooly is a combination of all the horny women I've known over the years.

Do you resent paying taxes?

Everyone needs a certain amount of income to survive, and people are getting taxed well below this level. As a single person with no dependents, income taxes kick in after the first $7,200 I earn. That strikes me as a bit low.

The thing that really bothers me is Social Security, which is really an ass-backwards graduated tax; above a certain income level, people don't pay any additional FICA [Social Security withholding tax]. And CEOs, whose wealth comes largely from stock options, only pay capital gains taxes when they exercise those options—no Social Security at all! Meanwhile, I'm dumping tons of cash every year into a system that's scheduled to run dry before I'm eligible to receive a penny. Clearly, we need several more tax brackets beyond the top one that currently exists and the wealthy need to pay into the Social Security system.

America: Best country ever?

Well, on one hand we produced Woody Allen. On the other, we've produced the worst food, worst architecture (plastic huts and corporate cubes), the most ridiculously huge cars in the world and we are anti-intellectual to the point of worshipping stupidity. It's your call.

Jen Sorensen, left, checking out another country in a trip to England in 2000.

Scott Bateman

Architect of deconstruction, he's revolutionizing the editorial cartoon format

38-year-old Portland resident and maniacal music fan Scott Bateman does for editorial cartooning what Gang of Four and Devo did to music—accepting no assumptions in an amazingly incestuous art form, he deconstructs and distills its simplest graphic elements for rapid consumption by a media-saturated public. His syndicated cartoons have appeared in *The New York Times, USA Today, Newsweek* and *Z* magazine.

TED RALL: Can political cartooning change the world? Obviously not. But can it change anything at all? Have *you* changed anything?

SCOTT BATEMAN: I think political cartoons influence opinion more than we think. So many people, when they look at their daily paper's opinion page, all they look at are the cartoons. They're not reading George Will or Molly Ivins, they're looking at the damn cartoons. This is why I'm disappointed that so many regular editorial cartoonists don't seem to aspire to do anything more than make a Jay Leno-y joke about some news item rather than try to further debate on some important topic. We have power because people are reading us.

I hear from readers all the time who say things like, "Thanks for that cartoon—I thought I was the only one who thought that way." So you know, just helping people not to feel crazy when they question things is a great effect to have.

Many of the artists in *Attitude* toil mainly in the world of the free alternative weekly press. You, on the other hand, are marketed by your syndicate to mainstream dailies. Does the fact that you use multiple panels and an unorthodox—non-Jeff McNelly-inspired—drawing style reduce the number of clients you might otherwise have?

Since 1997, I've been syndicated by King Features as part of their "Best & Wittiest" package. I'm not sure if I'm supposed to be "best" or "wittiest." B&W goes out to about 400 papers and features 12 cartoonists—11 of them are traditional, works-at-a-daily-paper-and-draws-kinda-like-MacNelly guys, and then there's me, with my pointy noses and funky hair shapes.

I'm still amazed that (a) I'm even syndicated in the first place, and (b) that so many papers that get the package actually use me quite a bit, more than they use some of the other guys in the package.

I'm not sure how many of these papers would want to buy my work if I were syndicated as my own Bateman product thing, so I'm very happy right now to be getting this kind of exposure.

You have a subtle but evident approach of deconstructing panels, toying with the concept of the panel itself. Is this intentional?

That is completely the plan, you bet. I started out by not drawing forehead lines in my profile shots. Then I started leaving out a lot of the panel lines. Now I've started a campaign against word balloons. I want to tear down as much as I can that is traditional in our field because it's so boring not to.

If you could be the absolute dictator of any country on earth, which one would you choose and how would you abuse your power?

You know, I don't need a whole damn

country. I'd be thrilled if I could afford a damn house someday. It doesn't even have to be a nice house. Just a roof and some walls. I'm not picky.

Uh-huh. But what's your fave country? And don't you have any ambition to exert control over your fellow human beings?

I've always liked Canada, for all the obvious reasons—nifty health care system, gun control, tasty beer, and MuchMusic's Sook Yin-Lee.

The only control I want to exert over my fellow human beings would be to instruct 99.9999 percent of them to leave me alone, and maybe to outlaw any clothing item promoting Tommy Hilfiger. If Tommy Hilfiger saw some of the people wearing his name in foot-high letters he'd change his name in a second, I'm sure.

Please describe the most traumatic event in your life so far.

No thanks.

Well, I went through a lot of trauma growing up through a series of divorces and single motherhood, living at the edge of the poverty line most of that time and still managing to get through high school and graduate from a decent college. And that struggle is still what's behind most of my political cartoon work to this day. And not just the personal strife of growing up in the '70's and early '80's—we also had to deal with the music of Journey, Foreigner, Loverboy and Night Ranger. And don't forget Styx, or you'll be doomed to repeat them. It was a dark, dark time, as you know.

I've also had a difficult time dealing with a sort of brain chemical imbalance thing that runs in my family. Because I was without health insurance most of the past ten years, I'd been unable to avail myself of the leaps in pharmaceutical technology in dealing with these kinds of problems and it really is like white-knuckling your way through every single day, laughing on the outside, screaming in terror on the inside, sometimes wanting to kill yourself because you can't get it together to simply go down to the grocery store to buy a damn loaf of bread because you know people on the street will all be looking at you. It's hard to talk about because if you haven't been through it, you just can't relate.

How do you expect to die?

I've always been fascinated by the human brain. One of the reasons I majored in psych in college was for the more medical side of it,

where we got to dissect sheep brains and stuff. It was awesome.

So I think, because of my brain obsession, I've always imagined that I would die from a brain tumor the size of a good-sized lime. Brain tumors are cool.

What do you think is the greatest challenge facing America in the 21st century?

The biggest challenge for the new century is going to be simply living through it. It's very likely that global warming will start making the world a super-gnarly place to try to live in a hundred years. I'm not sure if many people will be alive then. Fun, huh?

What makes you want to get up every day and do cartoons?

When I first became syndicated, I had this startling realization—I would be one of the few people who make under $15,000-a-year whose opinions could be seen in newspapers coast-to-coast on a fairly regular basis. You simply don't hear from people like me on most editorial pages most days. So it became my goal to basically cartoon about my life—to try to get across what it's like to be part of the lower middle class in this country, to work hard and still have no health insurance, to be just a few dollars away from having to declare bankruptcy month after month in an economy that was supposedly the greatest ever. To be a reality check in a media environment that ignores anyone who doesn't have a big stock portfolio and a giant SUV. And weirdly, I've found that the more personal I make my work, the more universal people think it is.

Like Feiffer, your cartoons often depict individuals who feel disconnected from publicized reality. Is that how you feel?

Like, totally. What I see in the media is so amazingly different from my actual daily experience, and the experiences of my friends and family—it's a huge disconnect, and that bit of cognitive dissonance is what fuels so much of my work.

You incorporate inorganic graphic elements—typeset headlines, dead lines laid down with rulers—with organic cartooning. The music you like, such as Stereolab and Kraftwerk, also blend the mechanical with the organic. What's up—are you some sort of crazy robot man?

Yes, I'm a killer cyborg from the 23rd century. Fear me. Fear me! Are you fearing me yet? OK, I'll wait...doot de doot doowah...

There are two reasons I rely so heavily on graphic design elements in my work. First, I have a graphic design background. I put myself through college doing graphic design work and after college did design work at Nike, and I continue to have a fascination with design which can't help but come out in my work. Second, I can't fucking draw, so rulers save my damn life.

You obviously don't have much faith in economists. Is economic activity fundamentally unpredictable?

Economists are full of shit. Their economic models are full of shit. Their predictions and analyses are full of shit. My job is to point out how full of shit they since no one else is really doing it. It's a public service, really.

Actually, there are some very good economists out there who actually have a damn clue. They're just never quoted in *The New York Times*, *The Washington Post* or CNN so people never get to hear a dissenting opinion about economic policy in this country.

I mean, look at what mainstream economists have gotten wrong over the past decade. The whole natural-level-of-unemployment theory's been blasted out of the water. They were shocked, shocked when a vastly overrated stock market started to fall. And look what they did to Russia's economy, to the detriment of millions of people. And that's just a small start. Bastards.

If invited to do so, would you ever watch an execution?

No, because I would try, futilely, to stop it. Capital punishment is barbaric and it doesn't work. We should trash it.

If it worked, could you get over the barbaric part?

No. It's a gruesome thing we as a society condone for some reason, and I don't understand why. I don't really want to watch anybody die. Well, maybe Carrot Top.

Are gay people born with a predisposition to homosexuality or do they learn it?

I love this whole thing the Right has, that we need to protect kids from gays or the kids will learn to be homosexual. Like, what, do they distribute textbooks and Barbra Streisand CDs? What is that? No,

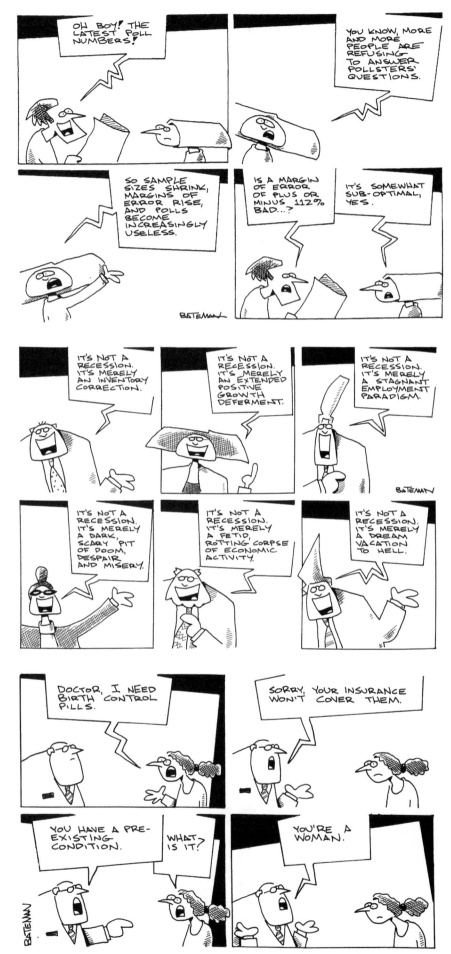

homosexuality is clearly something you're born with and really, sexual preference is just as silly a thing to judge people by as eye color or skin color.

Yeah, but we all know people who start out straight, come out as gay, and end up getting married again—or some other variant. Don't you think some people choose their sexual orientation for whatever reason? And if so, does it matter?

Sure, some people, I mean, OK, I like to think of it as a continuum, right? One end is "100 percent straight" and the other end is "100 percent gay," and everyone's born somewhere in the middle. Very few people are all the way up against either of the ends. Sometimes straight people are attracted to the same sex; sometimes gay folks are attracted to the opposite sex. A lot of folks are closer to the middle, attracted to either sex. It's all good and nobody should care that much. It's all natural and stuff.

What's the dumbest thing you've ever done?

In high school, I went to this huge outdoor concert called Oregon Jam. It featured Foreigner, Loverboy, Blue Oyster Cult, Triumph, and, in the opening slot, this new person, Joan Jett. I should have left after Joan Jett.

Honestly, exposure to either Loverboy or Foreigner for prolonged periods makes individual brain cells start committing suicide. It's a sad, terrible thing. Plus, I have to carry the visual of the lead singer guy from Loverboy's spandex bulge with me for the rest of my life. There isn't enough Paxil in the world to help with that.

Catch Scott in the middle of a creative frenzy or panicking before a deadline, live and online on the BateCam: www.batemania.com.

Tim Eagan

What do you do after running for District Attorney?
Crank out two comic strips every week!

Tim Eagan, 57, produces two alternative-weekly comics which appear in *The Santa Rosa Press Democrat, Funny Times, Comic Relief* and *Santa Cruz Comic News.* "Deep Cover" tackles politics and current events; "Subconscious Comics" is a post-psychedelic rumination on human insecurity—which is political in and of itself. He ran for district attorney in his cartooning mecca home town of Santa Cruz, California, was a regular on National Public Radio's "All Things Considered" and has taught himself enough carpentry to build his own house.

TED RALL: You're the secret weapon of alternative cartooning. You do two strips, "Deep Cover" and "Subconscious Comics," both of which are highly regarded but not widely distributed. Given how tight your drawing style and writing are, those who know about you can't figure out why you're not wealthy. What gives?

TIM EAGAN: I'd like to open that question up to a group discussion, if I may. Why aren't I rich, anyhow? I just hope I don't die before it's answered (or remedied).

You're also one of the oldest dudes in this book. (And I've got bad news for you: You're older than any of the chicks.) Yet here you are, doing work that appeals to twentysomethings that appears in publications read by twentysomethings. Do you ever feel generationally disconnected?

Generationally disconnected? Nah. Liberals are forever young. Although I still can't let go of that backward baseball cap thing. That, and labial studs. (Mom! What were you thinking?) The oldest? Really? This is a fun interview already! I am still in suitable shape for an open casket, though.

What's the difference between the two strips? Why don't you just do one strip twice as often?

The difference is pretty basic. "Subcon" is 99 percent current-events-free. "Deep Cover" is the opposite. "Subcon" dates back to '81, and I've had a hard time abandoning it even though its strange premise has kept it from being mainstream popular. It'll have to go some time, I think, even though I'll miss the place it takes me.

Tell our humble gathering about your day job. Is it really true that you ran for District Attorney?

I did. It was an instructive and entertaining experience to witness politics from the inside, if only in a tongue-partly-in-cheek mode. I styled myself at the time as a liberal/populist/libertarian. Predictably, the people loved it; I took over 15 percent of the vote with only the wispiest of war chests. I wish someone else would try that mix for real. I don't practice law any more. The real money, as we know, is in alternative cartooning.

Do you hang out with Clay Butler? Both of you guys live in Santa Cruz, and cartooning can be a pretty lonesome profession.

I like Clay's work, but we've never connected. Hold on, I'll e-mail him right now using the address on his strip...there! See? I'm not antisocial after all!

Who was the best president in American history? Who was worst?

I was nuts about TR [Teddy Roosevelt] as a youth and I still like him, but I mostly

admire the guys who didn't make it. Adlai Stevenson, Bobby Kennedy, and (God forgive him) Ralph Nader. The worst? I think W has a shot at it if his essential mean-spiritedness is given a chance to bloom. Nixon was a certified slimedog, of course, but there were some real chumps in the Oval Office in the early 19th century.

Back to the two-strip thing. Are there editors who, say, hate "Deep Cover" but love "Subconscious Comics" or vice versa?

Do editors actually talk to you? The ones that talk to me have said that "Subcon" was too weird for them. And a little icky, too, as I read between their lines. People who lead rich internal lives seem to like "Subcon." I'm afraid that includes a lot of hideously self-absorbed folks, as well. Many crazy people find that the strip is good therapy. S'okay with me; I can only hope that "Deep Cover" is therapeutic, too—for the body politic.

Did you like "Pulp Fiction"?

I liked the TV cut. I was afraid to see the cinematic version because I thought it might be too violent for my delicate sensibilities. I missed "A Clockwork Orange" for the same reason, even though I'm a Kubrick fan. The digressions in the script were very entertaining—like real life, only much better written.

Some of your cartoons concern themselves with aging. You're in your late fifties. What's it like? Is there anything I should know about the next 20 years?

Couldn't we call it mid-fifties? Anyway, let me just say that my days are filled with the pain and dread of advancing decrepitude. Endless fodder for humor, that. Actually, I'm finding that those macabre jokes about impending death are losing some of their power to amuse.

Who were your artistic and political influences?

Wally Wood. Great draftsman, and his drawings of voluptuous women were hot. Al Capp, ditto, though after I saw him on TV, I was less impressed. Complete nutbar. Later, I was even less impressed when I heard that Frazetta was doing his inking for him. Then came his trashing of Joan Baez, who was the genuine article, in my view. Oh well. J.P. Donleavy had a big effect on my writing style. As with most folks, my family had the greatest influence on my politics. Particularly in providing me with a healthy distrust for the powerful. Most

people steer clear of politics in polite social settings. My father charged in with a will. It did limit our social circle, I guess, but I still prefer talking with someone who isn't afraid to throw down the gauntlet of a pissant political opinion.

My wife wants to put a big tree in my apartment. A tree. With limbs and stuff.

But we only have 750 square feet, and I'm using them for other stuff. So I say no. Am I wrong?

One word: Bonsai!!! (But you've got to be there all the time.)

Your political cartoons are intelligent but rarely angry in that I-wish-you-

Candidate Eagan engages in mock political debate in a scene from "Campaign Comics," his low-budget campaign literature in a Quixiotic quest for the office of District Attorney.

were-all-dead-motherfuckers kind of way. It's more like you're really, really sad that people are so mean and stupid and short-sighted. Is that an accurate reflection of your worldview? Have you always been this way?

Good call. I've never been convinced that ripping out your enemies' guts actually accomplishes anything. Don't get me wrong; I have the urge to disembowel, but I try to use that impulse as fuel, not as a weapon. I confess that I'm trying to influence people's hearts and minds with my work. For me, though, just ranting doesn't get the job done.

As a liberal guy, can you imagine a series of events that might have transformed you into a conservative?

Nope. Liberal arrogance is so much more holy than conservative arrogance, don't you think? Besides, Grandpa was a Wobbly; can't forsake that.

> "I've never been convinced that ripping out your enemies' guts ... accomplishes anything. Don't get me wrong; I have the urge to disembowel, but I try to use that impulse as fuel, not as a weapon."

What's your favorite cartoon or comic strip?

I really was a big "L'il Abner" fan, but that one's history. Today (on the standard daily comics page, at least) my eyes go first to "Zits," "Doonesbury," "Mutts" and "Zippy." Of the alternatives, I most like "Tom the Dancing Bug."

What did you think of the Clinton Presidency?

I think the pop-psych analysis of him as a schizophrenic isn't far wrong. A lot of things I observe about him tells me he's a good boy: erect posture, respect for interpersonal nuance, smart as a whip, polite, folksy demeanor.

Then there's the phoniness: the biting of the lower lip and other transparent poses. To say nothing of all those irresistible impulses he is prey to. I will never forgive him for the welfare reform cave. I guess dead crack babies don't vote.

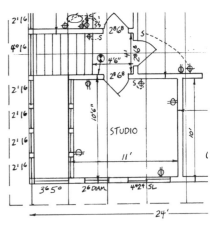

SECOND FLOOR PLAN
600 SQUARE FEET
¼" = 1'

Eagan's plans for the house he built.

If it was up to you, would paying off the national debt be a priority for you?

Yep. Maybe it's that late fifties thing, but it's a common sense issue for anybody who's ever been in debt. Pay that sucker off! Just so long as I can still buy those cool I-Bonds. All that tax revenue the anti-tax crazies claim is "our money"... well, isn't it "our debt," too? The irony is that this used to be one of the conservatives' (or at least the Republicans') big issues.

What's your take on abortion?

It's a difficult issue which most people will not discuss. Get angry, yes. Get self-righteous, yes. Really grapple with the issue, no. I guess I come down on the side of having power over one's own body and keeping the government out of wombs. Then I read about untold thousands of fetuses aborted in China and India simply because they are female. My gut tells me that is a bad thing.

Under what circumstances should Americans go to war?

Whenever that question comes up, I ask myself, "What would I be willing to die for?" It always comes up as "Not very many things." But those things are pretty worthy, I think. To keep myself from being killed. Same with my family and friends, and by extension, my country, I guess. I think I'd be willing to die to stop Burt Lancaster in "Seven Days in May." To stop the Holocaust, too. After, that, it

gets kinda fuzzy.

Why are almost all cartoonists white males?

Ooh, good question. Maybe Aaron McGruder [African-American creator of the daily strip "Boondocks"] will attract more black kids to cartooning. When I teach cartooning in junior high, the girls are no less talented than the boys, but I'm guessing girls still get more pressure to be "sensible" in their career choices and hence don't take such a chancy life path. And boys tend to live more dangerously (stupidly) anyway, right? Girls might also get pressure from their peers to avoid an "unfeminine" hobby. In Santa Cruz, at least, cartoonists are honored regardless of gender.

Which political cartoonists, mainstream and alternative (and hey, is there a difference anyway?) do you admire? How does a successful political cartoon distinguish itself?

Edward Sorel, David Suter, Tom Toles, Ralph Steadman and Clay Bennett are some of my mainstream favorites. I read "Doonesbury" every day. Everyone in this book is brilliant and underappreciated, of course. As to distinguishing characteristics, I think a distinctive drawing style helps. Drafting talent will get my attention, but it is the originality and insightfulness of a cartoonist's ideas that keep me coming back. Oh yeah, and the jokes.

Name your five favorite authors and why.

J.P. Donleavy's language, rhythm and humor are like food to me. Ursula LeGuin fills my sci-fi needs, and her characters are pretty solid. William Gibson gives me a kind of virtual, city-harsh consciousness I can't normally feel here in the woods. Flann O'Brien nourishes my love of language and lyricism. And you can't beat Edgar Allan Poe.

If you were sentenced to the rest of your life in prison, but were allowed to read, write and draw, how would you spend that time? Would you kill yourself?

Kill myself? Jeepers, Ted! Do I have to choose just one between reading, writing and drawing? Maybe I'd take up sculpture if it were just me and those four walls. Or do my own "Live! From the Big House" radio show.

   Come to think of it, prison might be a real gas!

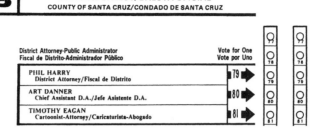

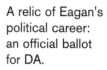

A relic of Eagan's political career: an official ballot for DA.

Derf

Jeffrey Dahmer's classmate on piercings, generational politics and yes, Jeffrey

Though Derf's "The City" runs in more than 60 weekly papers, including the *Chicago Reader, Philadelphia Weekly, New Times Los Angeles* and *Washington City Paper,* the success of his visceral graphic assaults on American pop culture, generational politics and all things piercing cannot overshadow the fact that he went to high school with notorious serial-killer/cannibal Jeffrey Dahmer in a small town near Akron, Ohio. His graphic-novel memoir of a year spent working the back of a garbage truck between high school and college, *Trashed,* was recently published by Slave Labor Graphics.

TED RALL: Warning: You are now about to be asked the stupidest of all questions asked of cartoonists. I am not talking about the infamous 'Where Do You Get Your Ideas?' query. No. I am, in fact, about to ask—warning! warning!—what are your artistic influences? Unlike most of the people in this book, your style doesn't spring from the loins of Crumb or Marvel or *Mad* or whatever, or maybe it does, but if it does it just ain't obvious. So whose drawing styles do you admire and look to for guidance?

DERF: Well, I would happily rip off Crumb... If I could draw that well. But aaaaaaall those little scratchy lines....brrrrrrrr. I'd get bored after one panel. I'm just not that obsessive. I grew up liking a hodgepodge of greats: Crumb, Ed

"Big Daddy" Roth, Vaughn Bode, Basil Wolverton, Don Martin, Ron Cobb (the great hippie political cartoonist) even fan cartoonist Don Rosa. I'd imitate each of them for awhile, get dissatisfied with the result, then move on to the next one. But I didn't find my way stylistically until I stopped reading cartoons in the mid-'80's. Sold all my cartoon books and just went cold turkey. That sounds unnecessarily extreme but it worked. I started looking for inspiration elsewhere, particularly in the postpunk imagery of the day—posters, handbills, that sort of thing.

Then I became very interested in the Expressionist movement of the early 20th century, particularly the Germans (I was studying German at the time) like Georg Grosz, Max Beckmann, Frans Masereel and Otto Dix. That was the inspiration for

the heavy jagged lines and twisted perspective. So my style is really just punk cartoons filtered through an expressionistic lens. That sounds a lot more intellectual than it really is.

You obviously have an unnatural attraction and/or interest in piercings, tattoos, body hair and other body-altering techniques favored by twentysomethings and aging Gen Xers. How much of your body is

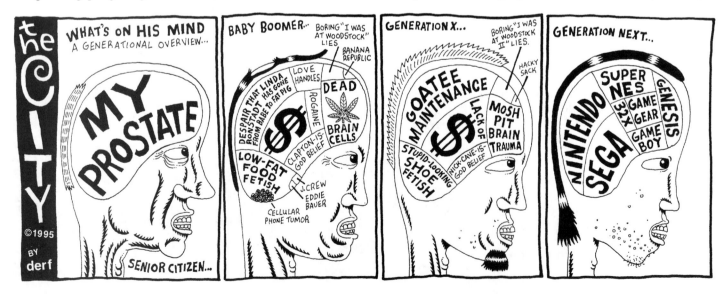

affected by such things? Why do these topics come up in your work so much?

I know, I know. Actually I've really gotten away from that stuff. But those old cartoons on piercing keep circulating and I can't shake the rep. Lately, I've been doing toons on how pathetic and boring the fad is. I'm biding my time until Generation Y comes up with its own idiotic fashion and then we can begin again.

You've obviously thought a lot about generational politics and distinctions. What do you think about the argument that generations are inherently arbitrary and meaningless? What do you think about what comes after Us, Us being Gen Xers? Will they destroy us all? And if so, would that be a good thing?

> "I draw what I see. Maybe that's just the Cleveland gene pool. You mean people don't look this way?"

A-ha! But I'm not Gen X. I'm from the now-forgotten and numerically insignificant Blank Generation, which came of age in the late '70's and brought the world punk rock and Reagan Youth [not the early '80's hardcore band, but that era's young conservatives whom the band's name lampooned]. We never did manage to cut through the cultural fart of the Baby Boom and then were swept into oblivion by an avalanche of Xers. I think we had about two months of glory in 1977 and that was that. Being sandwiched between those two demographic monstrosities is the very reason I do dwell on generational interplay. It's a great objective vantage point. If I had to pick sides however, I'm more sympathetic to Gen X, while freely admitting that the Boomers had more fun than the rest of us combined.

Your strip is called "The City," but you live in Cleveland. What's up with that?

Cleveland isn't a city?

You may draw the most physiologically-unappealing characters in alternative cartooning. Do you actually see everybody like that or what?

I draw what I see. Maybe that's just the Cleveland gene pool. You mean people don't look this way? Hmmmmm.

What's the source for your "True Story" tales? Do you, Scott Adams-like, ask your readers to send them in? Are they collected from friends? Or do you really have the bad luck to have all that shit happen to you personally? And if the latter is affirmative, is it a Cleveland thing?

I do get stories sent in by readers, unsolicited (and unpaid) but greatly appreciated. Others come from friends and

family. Probably about half of them have been personally witnessed by myself and hastily written down on napkins or receipts. They're great fun to do. Good excuse to spend a nice day walking the streets.

If you were appointed Emperor For a Day, what three things/laws/habits about the United States would you change?

(1) Coffee sizes by law must be called small, medium and large... no Latin, no "extra-large" or "big-ass huge."

(2) All Wal-Marts can be no bigger than 20 feet square.

(3) Wall Street traders must wear Mexican wrestling masks during work hours.

If you could wish that any celebrity had never been born, who would it be and why?

Celine Dion. Because she's too damn loud.

OK, I've waited long enough for this. You went to high school with serial killer Jeffrey Dahmer. You were friends. Were there any hints of his future dining habits back then? Do you think he's guilty? How did you feel when he was murdered himself in prison? Obviously: What was he like? And, the dumb one: How, if at all, did this experience affect your world view and/or your work?

My wife was a reporter for the local paper and when the Dahmer story broke, she called me and said someone I graduated with had killed and dismembered a bunch of people. Dahmer was my second guess.

So, yeah, he was a freak...but there were lots of freaks, as there are in any

> "[My wife] said someone I graduated with had killed and dismembered a bunch of people. Dahmer was my second guess."

DAHMER AS A TELEPHONE POLE

DAHMER AS A BAG OF GROCERIES

Contemporary drawing of high school classmate Jeffrey Dahmer.

school. I dunno, every little episode, looking back on it, takes on such heavy portend, knowing what we now know. I actually consider Dahmer a tragic figure. That statement always freaks people out. But I think that he could have been saved, but he wasn't because at every crucial step of his descent into hell the adults in his life—parents, teachers, authorities—failed him. If he'd been caught just once early on...for instance when he was drunk at school at 7:30 am or when he tried to dig up the body of a classmate who was killed in an accident, then all those people would never have been slaughtered. I'm not saying Dahmer still wouldn't have been dysfunctional, but it would've been the difference between him living unemployed in his mom's basement and eating bod-

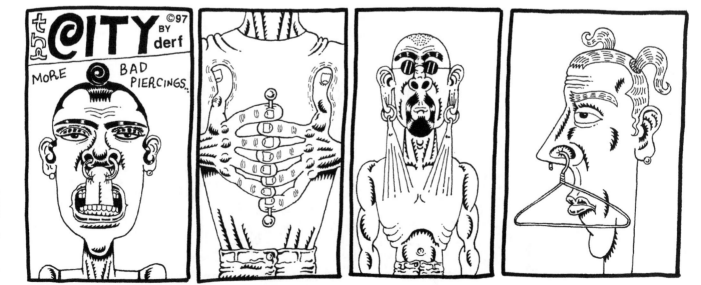

ies in Milwaukee.

I don't know what effect it had on me. I don't think you rub elbows with malevolent evil and walk away unscathed. Was I ever in danger? Who knows. I know the body of his first victim was in his house when I and my friends were around that summer after graduation. Might have even been in the trunk of his car about five feet away. We've all lost sleep over that. But at this point, I've dealt with it.

I just finished a comic book [the self-published *My Friend Dahmer*, for sale through Derf's website] about going to high school with Dahmer, mainly to answer all questions about Dahmer. When asked in the future, I'll just hand someone a copy of the comic and that will be that.

You complain a lot about all things American. Which country or countries has more of a clue about things than we do?

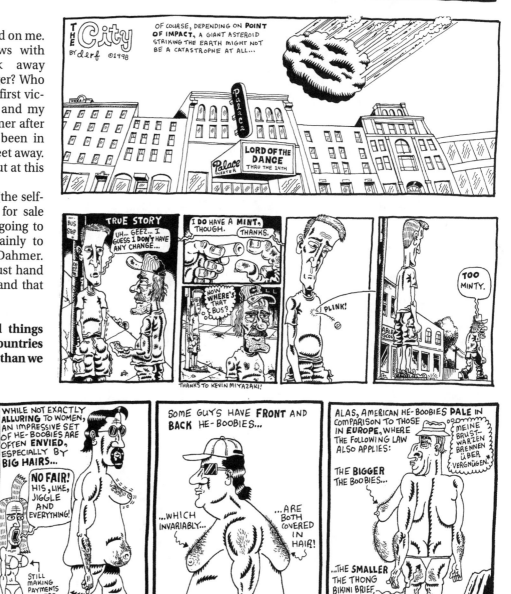

Derf and his brother in 1966 Akron, Ohio. Derf is the one packing heat.

Canada. I love Canada. Theirs is a far more advanced civilization. I keep encouraging them—using my soapbox in a Toronto paper—to sweep down from the north and wipe this wretched society off the map. Alas, they don't seem to have the motivation. You'd think they'd at least invade Maine as a test. It's not as if anyone outside of that state would notice.

You're obviously down on advertising. But without ads, there'd be no weekly newspapers and thus no "The City." You'd be wearing a suit in some bank! So: Want to reconsider that?

Well, I've never objected to sex ads.... and that's about 90 percent of ad content in your typical weeklies.

For which presidential candidate did you vote in 1992? 1996? 2000?

1992: Gus Hall, because someone had to vote for the old commie. 1996: Nader. 2000: Scrappy Doo.

One of the angrier cartoons I've seen of

yours is the post-election coup d'état piece where an "obscure cartoonist" is being dragged off by government goons. Why did the Florida debacle anger you so much?

Actually, it didn't. I found it fascinating. Since I am equally disgusted by both parties, I had no emotional investment in the outcome, but clearly Bush did not win, not even a clear victory in the electoral vote. And since he clearly lost the popular vote, he's a usurper. What bugs me is how his handlers are trying to pass him off as legit, as if he has some kind of mandate just because they say so. That particular cartoon was one of those magical ones that just write themselves. You wouldn't believe the mail that thing got. Bush supporters are unsurpassed in their paranoia. They know their boy is a fraud and their answer is to shout down anyone who raises that point.

I should point out that I'm not really a political cartoonist. I'm a cartoonist who frequently does political humor. There's a difference there. I have no requirement to comment on the issue of the week, nor do I have any delusion whatsoever that I'm swaying public opinion or changing the world. I'm in it purely for the laughs, man. I don't write anything I don't believe in, but it's gotta be funny first and foremost. I figure if I get to the end of my life and can say I made people laugh for a few seconds a week... well, hey, that's not a bad legacy.

Tried illegal drugs? Which ones did you like and why?

Nothing hard. Pot, mostly... purely in social settings. Shrooms. Peyote. Purty

colors. All in my younger days. I do have a six-foot-high Turkish water pipe next to my drawing board, but I use it only to hold my brushes.

Have you ever been an earnest sign-waving protester type? Are you now?

I'm a ranter, but not a participant. Typical cartoonist. Watching from the sidelines, scribbling madly away.

Why do you use that long horizontal format? "The City" could run as a comic strip—has it ever run on a comics page?

Good question, for which I have no real answer. When I created the strip in 1989 there weren't all that many weekly cartoons and, at that time, the papers themselves differed greatly in size and format.

Actually, I originally designed the strip to run either as a horizontal or as vertical, with two panels stacked on top of the other two. But no one ever ran it that way, so a horizontal it became forevermore. And, no... no daily paper has EVER run my stuff.

What is the one cartooning gig you'd kill for?

Backing up Vaughn Bode in groupie sex.

Punk buttons, top, from Derf's lapel, circa 1979, and his membership card from the "Big Daddy" Roth-inspired Mouse Monster Club.

Lalo Alcaraz

"La Cucaracha's" devastating blend of anarchic humor and vitriol, East LA-style

L alo Alcaraz draws "La Cucaracha" for *LA Weekly*, which is also syndicated through Universal Press Syndicate to the *Boston Globe* and *Dallas Morning News.* Though he focuses on such topics as discrimination against Latinos and other minorities, Alcaraz, 37, devotes equal time to savaging the stupid and the mean among those groups as well. Working out of the racial cauldron and melting-pot of Los Angeles, Alcaraz's most-recent book was *Latino USA,* a graphic novel-format history of the American Hispanic experience by Ilan Stavans which he illustrated.

TED RALL: You've carved out an interesting niche as a politically-conscious Latino cartoonist. But unlike most politically-conscious types, you don't take yourself too seriously. Is that just a pose to make people like you or is it for real? Or am I wrong about you not taking yourself too seriously?

LALO ALCARAZ: I take seriously my self-defined mission to be an advocate for Chicanos/Latinos and immigrants, not to mention people of color. I don't think I'm some kind of a crusader, I'm just a responsible Chicano—by definition, a Chicano is a politically-conscious and self-aware Mexican-American, so I'm just continuing a tradition of political advocacy and self-defense on behalf of my community.

Content-wise, I feel my work is a departure from the usual Chicano art that can be a bit didactic, preachy, bombastic, etc. I am consciously trying to extend Chicano art into editorial cartooning. We all know editorial cartooning is propaganda, so if I'm a good propagandist for the defense of Chicanos, etc., so be it. But as far as not really taking myself seriously, I feel it is the fact that I can tweak Latinos too and the fact that I can use non-PC language and imagery to attack everybody on any side of an issue — that is liberating.

Has your work always used your ethnicity as a focus or did that come about gradually? Could you be the same cartoonist if you were white?

In college, I was an edito-

SMALLPOX INFESTED BLANKETS! THANK YOU, JOHN SMITH!

LALO ALCARAZ ©1995

rial cartoonist for my school paper, *The Daily Aztec,* if you can believe that. It wasn't the Chicano paper; it was the SDSU paper. I did straight, news-oriented editorial cartoons. Occasionally, my Chicano background snuck in to the toons simply because I might do a César Chavez toon about how the School Student Board was too stupidly racist to allow him to speak on campus or other anti-frat toons on how they were so racist in doing fund-raisers for poor Tijuana kid charities—dressed in sombreros and begging with tin cups! So it depended on the subject matter.

Earlier, when I first started at the *LA Weekly,* I did purely militant Chicano cartoons, which was appropriate for the time and for me. They have transformed over time, as Latinos have become such a major part of life in the US. Now that I do daily paper-oriented editorial cartoons, it's back to the topics being out there. There's always some kind of Latino story/issue out in the press, so it's easy to focus on just topics directly affecting Latinos, although most issues affect everyone in some way.

If I was white, I could still be an advocate for Latinos or the downtrodden or whatever, but I would definitely not be able to be a direct voice to the Latino experience. That would be like the time a major newspaper syndicate tried to do a Latino-themed comic strip by a white cartoonist. People found out and the strip got canned. That is called brownfacing.

You're a Latino cartoonist, but your work is in English. And when you do stuff in Spanish, you provide English translations. Have you considered doing your work exclusively in Spanish for Spanish-language newspapers or have you done work like that in the past?

Yeah, just because I'm a Latino cartoonist doesn't mean I'm a foreigner, I was born here, dang! But seriously, I used to draw informally for an international toon syndicate based in New York and the way they could market me was as a foreign cartoonist. Domestic, as it were—Latinos are invisible. It is more like the concept of foreign Latinos doesn't tax one's Anglo brain and presuppositions too much.

I'd say it's mainly in Spanglish since I allow myself the freedom to write the cartoons with dialogue or phrasing I might use in my day-to-day life. I have done exclusively Spanish editorial cartoons for *La Opinion* in LA for about a year, but the section got canned.

Now I translate my toons into Spanish, which is both limiting but helps me avoid punnery in the original English, but this helps sales, man, as there are not a whole lot of US-based Spanish-language editorial cartoonists working out there, so I tried to cover topics of interest to the Spanish language readership.

Bilingual education is a big issue in California, where you live. Most left-of-center types favor joint teaching of Spanish and English in public schools. Do you? And if so, what would you say to the argument that children need to learn English first and foremost to get by in American society? After all, you'd have a hard time making it in Kazakhstan if you didn't focus on learning Kazakh.

This is the only country in the world where people want to strip kids of knowledge they enter school with, i.e., non-English languages. Also, there's got to be plenty of upper-class Kazakhs—purely for example here—that are fluent in some other language, say French or Russian or something, no? Kids here pick up English naturally and can do so

in the class room and playground, I have never met this supposed Latino that doesn't want to learn English, everybody wants to learn English, why can't they keep Spanish too? Why can't bilingualism be seen as an extra resource? Is it because kids who can think in two languages are smarter? Can't have extra-smart brown kids running around here; who would pick after white middle-class consumers, after all?

The anti-bilingual camp is very much in line with the Indian schools of the last century, where Native American culture would be stripped from native kids in order to make them easier to manage.

Your cartoons have never been angrier than during the controversy over Proposition 187, an anti-illegal immigration measure that ultimately was overturned by the Supreme Court as unconstitutional. Please explain Prop 187, your thoughts on it, and tell our readers whether every Californian who voted for 187 is a racist scumbag.

When you attack and condemn a person purely for who he or she is, you are a scumbag. That is wrong, and it's wrong against gays, women, blacks, etc. The proponents of 187, which would deny basic healthcare and public services for undocumented immigrants, was a spiteful and vindictive attack on immigrants and their kids, mainly brown-skinned Latino kids. They wanted teachers and other students to report on their undocumented classmates; what kind of Nazi shit is that? How many steps away are you from detention camps? It was scapegoating at its worst. I don't know if all pro-187 voters are racist scumbags but if they weren't, they were ignorant dumbshits and they don't understand the ramifications of what they were approving.

Why is your strip named "The Cockroach"?

"La Cucaracha" is taken from the Mexican Revolutionary-era ditty of the same title composed for the troop transports used by [Pancho] Villa's men, basically jalopies that often broke down. Also, cucarachas have been associated with poor people, i.e. poor Latinos, Mexicans, etc., and has often been appropriated in literature to symbolize a people that cannot be exterminated. The cucaracha will always be around and will survive you and me and all of our offspring, so goes the cliché. We are survivors. There: I said it.

The funny thing is when occasionally a narrow-minded Chicano or Hispanic will complain and howl about the use of the cucaracha in my work, but they are so worried about what white people will think, they forget to look into their own culture or to use critical thought and

really see what I'm trying to do. Ignorance is bliss, and many Latinos tend to be a really blissful people.

Most US cartoonists, including those in this book, are white. Why do you think that is? Did you have some formative experience as a kid that introduced you to comics that was different than most Latinos? Anyway, comics are hugely popular in the Spanish-speaking world—so what's up?

I think it's a function of having to survive this far growing up as a poor uneducated Mexican immigrant's kid. I barely got out of my barrio to get into college. I'm just a guy who was predisposed to be a cartoonist, who happened to make it through all the bullshit that comes with being poor and brown.

Many of my childhood friends are in jail or dead—so goes the cliché. Or they have six kids and a low-paying job. Hardly any of them graduated high school, even.

So that's not why I'm a cartoonist. In Mexico, there's an inordinate amount of cartoonists and a ton of excellent political cartoonists, so it's kind of a blood thing. Artistic talent runs in my family but I'm still waiting for my share. Basically, I dug *Mad* magazine, my brain is wired to mock, and *Mad* just confirmed my world view since I was a kid.

What's your favorite book?

Uh, is *Mad* magazine a book? Geez, the last whole book I actually read was either "Primary Colors" or "Rush Limbaugh is a Big Fat Idiot." Oh, I know, "Woodcuts of Women" by "Dagoberto Gilb."

Your style veers wildly between high abstraction a la "Dilbert"/"Life in Hell" and detailed caricature. How do you decide which approach to use in a given comic or a given character?

Hmm, yeah, I'm still working on my style, but it's definitely coming in at somewhere in between, leaning towards the realistic a bit. I think since I'm now working on a daily comic strip, the simple "Life in Hell" look is much easier to draw repetitively, so I'm sharpening my simplifying skills.

Usually, a nice defined caricature works to draw a highly-recognized figure but I find after a few times I get tired of drawing so many details, so I figure a way to do a simple caricature.

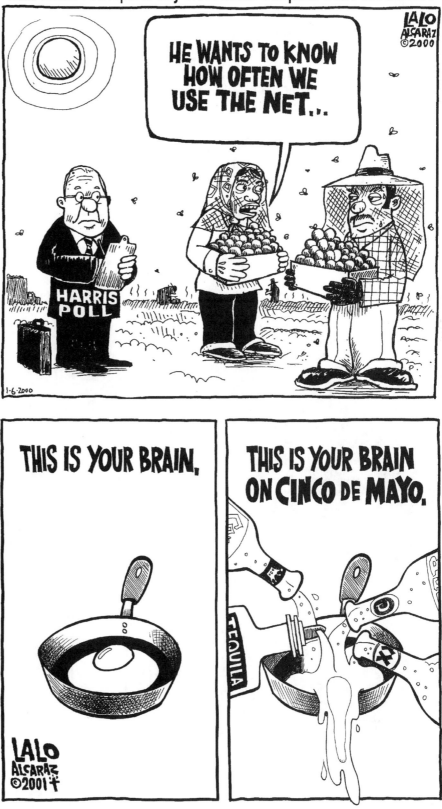

Does "La Cucaracha" pay well enough to support you and your family, or do you do other stuff too?

I draw cartoons and write columns and screenplays, and am developing "La Cucaracha" for both a daily comic and an animated TV show with a major producer of primetime animation.

Why do you think so many white Californians are so pissed at people of

Mexican ancestry? It's confusing to a non-Californian—all the coolest aspects of California culture, like the architecture and food, derive from Mexico. So what's the deal — really?

It's even more confusing to be a Mexican Californian! Throw in lots of the hard labor and service-industry jobs done by Latinos, and the ungratefulness is staggering. It seems familiarity does breed contempt, throw in the internal colony model and you got a recipe for racial oppression, economic segregation and fun fun fun!

What's the best country in the whole world?

Aztlan.

What's that?

Aztlan is the mythical homeland of the Aztecs, you know, my indigenous ancestors. In classic Chicano ideology, Aztlan is the Southwest, as the Aztecs claimed that they came from the North before they took root in the Valley of Mexico and evolved into the badass tribe they became. Aztec lore has it that the Aztecs would one day return to Aztlan and a good time would be had by all. So now, Aztlan signifies both a literal and symbolic takeover or re-taking of the Southwest by brown people. Seen the Census figures lately?

Should we spend billions to send a manned mission to Mars?

Sure, I'm a science freak and an inept amateur astrophysicist, so I'm into that. Just make sure I can get 40 acres and a Martian mule some time after we land.

Name your least-favorite board game.

Snakes and Ladders? Only because my three-year-old daughter makes me play it with her.

Describe your strangest first date.

Hmmm. I picked my wife up in a fight in my apartment in Berkeley. She attacked one of my friends who was taking smack. That was the first time I held her in my arms—sniff! So romantic. So I literally I had to pick her up and run into my bedroom with her to get her away from the brawl. She hated me in college, but I wore her down with my lack of charm, and now I've forced her to bear my unruly children.

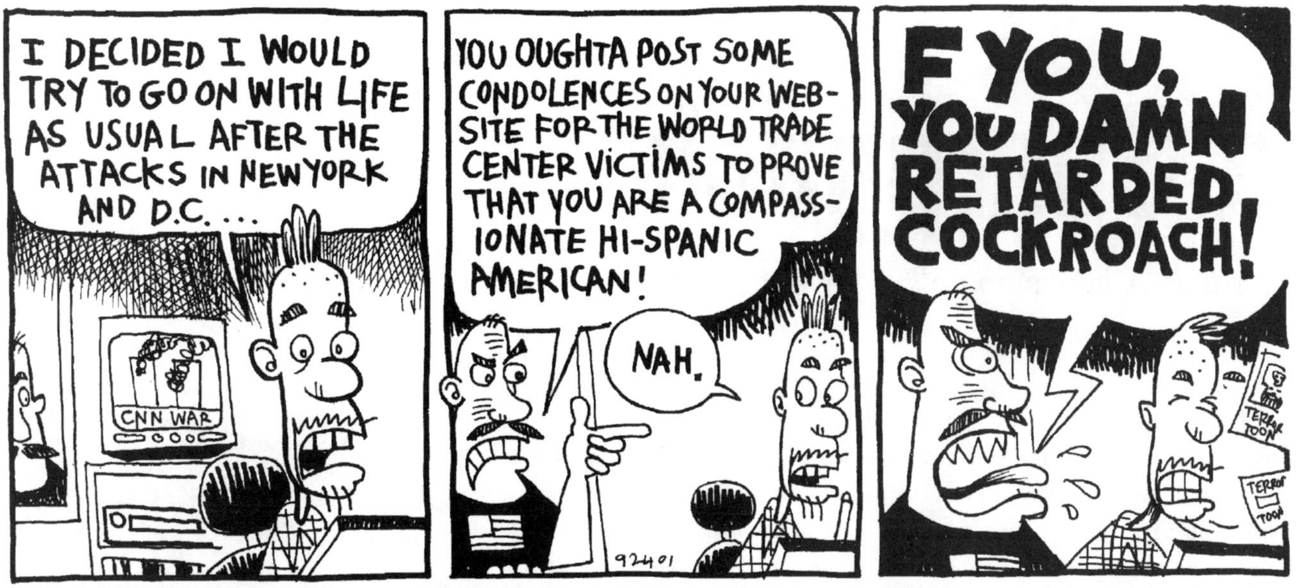
I DECIDED I WOULD TRY TO GO ON WITH LIFE AS USUAL AFTER THE ATTACKS IN NEW YORK AND D.C. ...
CNN WAR
YOU OUGHTA POST SOME CONDOLENCES ON YOUR WEB-SITE FOR THE WORLD TRADE CENTER VICTIMS TO PROVE THAT YOU ARE A COMPASS-IONATE HI-SPANIC AMERICAN!
NAH.
F YOU, YOU DAMN RETARDED COCKROACH!

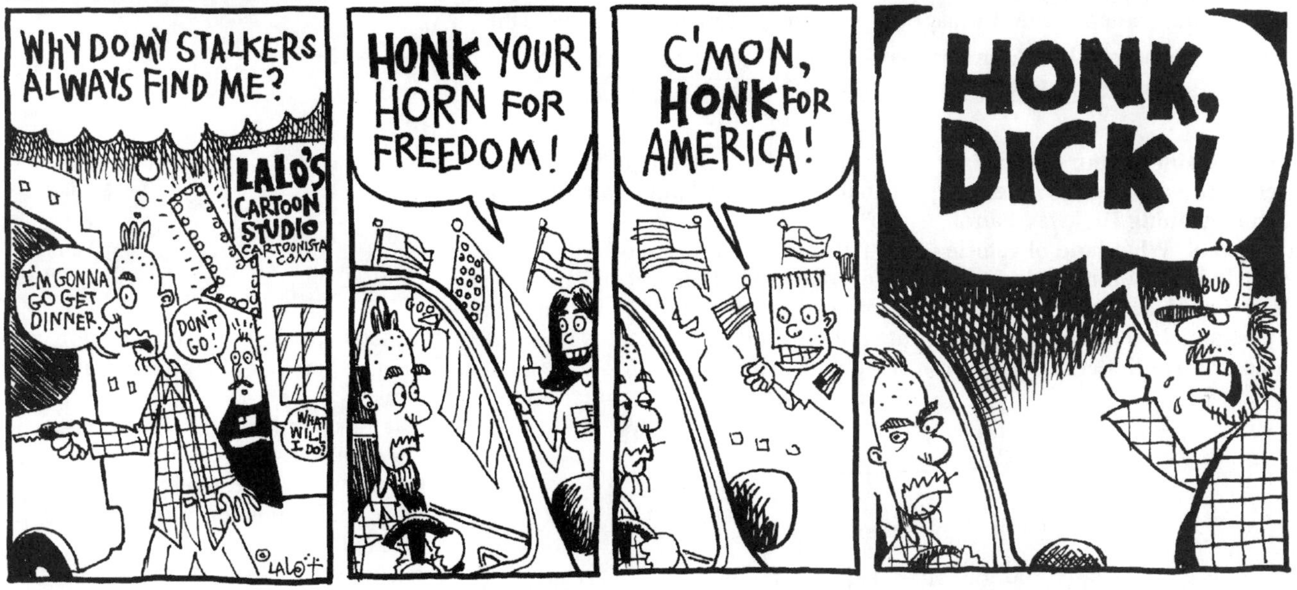
WHY DO MY STALKERS ALWAYS FIND ME?
LALO'S CARTOON STUDIO CARTOONISTA .COM
I'M GONNA GO GET DINNER.
DON'T GO!
WHAT WILL I DO?
HONK YOUR HORN FOR FREEDOM!
C'MON, HONK FOR AMERICA!
HONK, DICK!
BUD

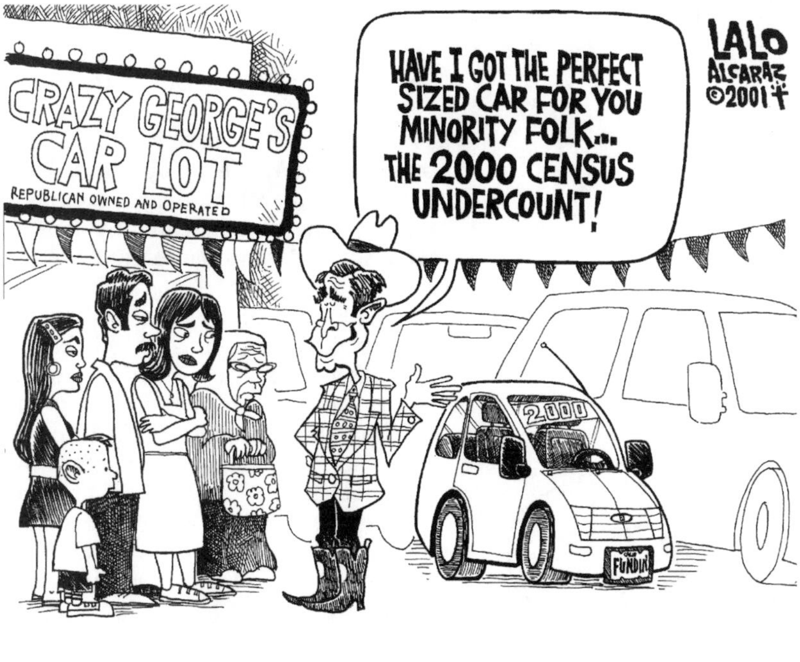
CRAZY GEORGE'S CAR LOT
REPUBLICAN OWNED AND OPERATED
HAVE I GOT THE PERFECT SIZED CAR FOR YOU MINORITY FOLK... THE 2000 CENSUS UNDERCOUNT!
LALO ALCARAZ ©2001
2000

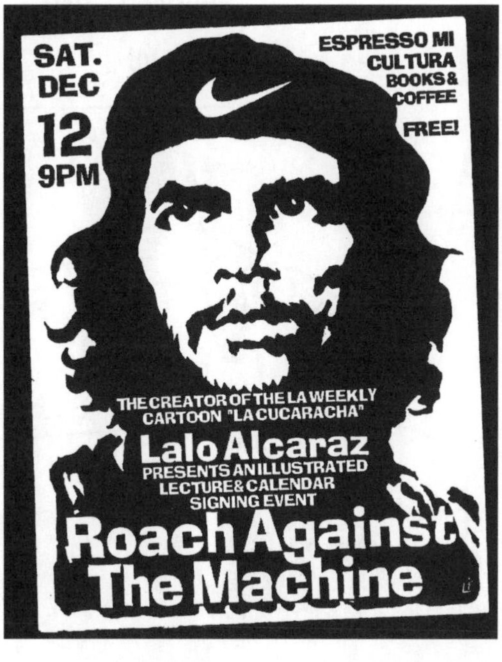
SAT. DEC 12 9PM
ESPRESSO MI CULTURA BOOKS & COFFEE
FREE!
THE CREATOR OF THE LA WEEKLY CARTOON "LA CUCARACHA"
Lalo Alcaraz
PRESENTS AN ILLUSTRATED LECTURE & CALENDAR SIGNING EVENT
Roach Against The Machine

Joe Sharpnack

Wickedly subtle assaults on political wrongdoers and the folks who vote for them

Any compendium of alternative political cartoonists must include an artist whose work is less "alternative" than the others. In this collection, Joe Sharpnack is that person. The 40-year-old Iowan draws single-panel editorial cartoons that include labels, donkeys and elephants—at first glance, hallmarks of mainstream edit-toon styles. Unlike his big-paper peers, however, the work Sharpnack produces for the *Iowa City Gazette* stands out for its passionate stances and subtly unusual approaches. He may be a "mainstream" cartoonist, but only to the extent that his sly anger harkens back to an era when the form favored strident opinion over empty jokes about the news—and that makes him "alternative" enough for *Attitude.*

TED RALL: You claim in your official bio that you were clocked doing 128 miles per hour past the Wyoming Highway Patrol. Do you have proof? What kind of vehicle were you driving? How long did it take you to stop? Can I get such a vehicle myself? My personal record is 115 mph, set in a school zone in Kettering, Ohio, in a '74 Nova.

JOE SHARPNACK: A school zone, Ted? A school zone?! What kind of a monster are you?!

In my bio, I said we got off with a ticket. I never identified myself as the driver. And no, I can't prove it. Traffic violations are not the kind of documents I keep in a scrapbook to brag about in later years. I'm afraid, however, that I must include myself in this youthful indiscretion in that the troopers had their guns drawn on all of us.

It took a little while to pull over because once we passed the patrol car we decided to outrun it. Eventually we agreed that there could be no outrunning a radio and decided to stop.

The vehicle was a stock '78 Dodge Magnum automatic, I think it had a 318 or 440 with a four-barrel. You really don't need that much power to bury a speedometer. I once did 120 in a six-cylinder '72 Plymouth Gold Duster. Go Mopar!

You're one of this book's more eclectic personalities. You're a playwright, drummer and former ditch-digger. Is cartooning one item from a menu for you or is it What You've Always Wanted To Do?

Cartooning is definitely my main source of income and time input, but I still keep all that other stuff alive regularly. Actually, I always wanted to be an astronaut but then found out how much damn math you had to know. I did want to be a full-time musician though, and that worked out for years until it became so monotonous I felt like I was carrying a lunchbox and clocking-in at the factory every night. Then I worked in factories and farms and plumbing and

SHARPNACK
© 2000 THE GAZETTE, IOWA CITY

The reason I stopped you sir, is because I noticed you weren't in jail.

drywall, etc., etc. Cartooning is what I decided to do after doing everything else.

I started thinking seriously about getting into cartooning when I was working in Nashville as a sort of "relief-pitcher" drummer for one of the major studios there. One morning, me and my friend Art were sitting around someone's kitchen table nursing galactic-class hangovers when Art noticed me depicting the previous evenings' debauchery on a napkin. "Jeez Joe, you ought to be a cartoonist," he said. "Yeah," I thought, "haven't tried that one yet."

Tell me what really, really pisses you off.

It's got to be the medical industry. Greed, greed and more greed. What kind of a person makes his fortune off someone else's misery? There's not another industrialized nation on earth that doesn't provide their citizens affordable (if not free) access to medical treatment. The insatiable lust for cash by doctors in this country borders on psychosis.

We don't need much more proof of this than the flood of bribe money that went into the pockets of Congress to kill the '93 Clinton health care plan (the majority of which was funded by the AMA...yes, they spent even more than the insurance companies). Medicine is as corrupt in this country as a Mexican drug cartel. Mortality blackmail is about as low as any human being can get.

Your work is done in classic editorial cartoon format, horizontal with some labels and even cross-hatching. Yet your peers consider you a denizen of the alternative world. Where do you think you fit? What makes an editorial cartoon mainstream versus alternative?

I trained myself in a more traditional style because editors kept saying, "Well y'know Joe, this stuff doesn't really look like an editorial cartoon" (i.e., [Jeff] MacNelly or [Pat] Oliphant). Given the attitudes of the times, I stuck to a more "traditional" style because I thought it would help market my material. And it did. It doesn't matter to me how someone draws or what conventions (if any) are employed; what's important is the message you convey. Since my career has become a bit more stable in the last few years, I've been going back to a style that's more independent and recognizable as my own.

Visually my work has become a lot simpler. I never understood why I needed to put a flower pot on the kitchen table when it clearly served no advantage in advancing the point of the cartoon. I've lost plenty (if not all) of the cross-hatching and have even coined the term "post-hatch" for myself and other cartoonists who have or are going back to a more individual and simplistic style.

As far as where I fit into traditional versus alternative, I've never distinguished myself as one or the other. If speaking out about issues that affect people's lives or focusing on things that are truly relevant puts me in the alternative camp, then I'm more than proud to wear that distinction even though very few "zine" type publications have ever run my work. "Well y'know Joe, this doesn't really look like an alternative cartoon..." Most of the publications that run my work are mainstream—the last holdouts who still want to engage their readers with the real root of an issue.

If you had to live in any century, 1st through 19th, which one would you select and where?

Early 19th century, Hannibal, Missouri.

Much of your work focuses on race issues. Do you believe that race relations is still the greatest problem facing the country? Is there a solution?

I don't think race relations are the biggest problem our country faces—but it's a doozy. It is, however, manageable.

Here's a little story: The junior high I attended was probably around 40 percent Hispanic, 59 percent Caucasian and a black guy. Since everyone pretty much lived in the same neighborhood, we all knew each other. Because of this, race was not really an issue. People were simply your neighbors and most folks got along fine. Such familiarity diffused a ton of situations that could have easily escalated into race-baiting street skirmishes had we all lived in segregated neighborhoods. Not to say that our school didn't have plenty of problems concerning violence. Most of the kids came from homes that were not exactly opulent, and, as a rule, poverty is the biggest catalyst of violent behavior that there is. There were fights at school every single day. Many small groups (we probably would've been labeled 'gangs' by today's standards) took to arming ourselves with knives, lead pipes, etc. (guns weren't in vogue—it wasn't chivalrous) because we were sick of being hassled. Our little bands, however, were not drawn exclusively upon racial lines. We were (hopefully) protecting ourselves against the assholes, not particular groups defined by physical characteristics. Remember, we all knew each other; we were pointing out collections of individuals as the source of our anxiety, not a faceless group of: (a) Mexicans (b) honkeys or (c) the black guy (who never bothered anyone, but it's just fun to throw him in the demographic mix for diversity's sake).

At the end of the day you could occasionally find the dad of Rolo, "leader" of the "Chicano Falcons" (or something) having a beer with the dad of Noodles, "leader" of the "Spikes" (or something) in their backyard discussing a plan to knock some sense into these stupid kids. And they did. Had these dads lived in separate parts of town, these meetings may never have taken place.

I hope that it's obvious in this example

Jackpot Sloakum—who bears a striking resemblance to Joe Sharpnack—spins his western yarns on stage with Oink Henderson and the Squealers.

that it all really comes down to economics. I don't care if everybody in your city is plaid, if they're poor, there's gonna be trouble.

I think if there is any progress to be made on the racial front, it lies in integration. People have to know each other. If the well-to-do keep fleeing to the suburbs (or even farther out) our chances for any kind of meaningful understanding of each other is lost.

What's more effective: local-issue or national cartoons?

I'm fairly secure in the notion that I will not be slapped with a defamation-of-character suit by Vladmir Putin. However, bring up the fact that a suburban Chicago mayor has a vaguely-written policy about not selling homes to blacks and boy, does the fur fly. Point out that a certain Iowa governor (not current) may be a little too cozy with anti-abortion forces and you get your taxes audited. Nothing hits home like a home-grown cartoon. Local cartooning has the most impact I've ever seen. This is where you can really do some good. The local level is where the debates that affect people on the most intimate level occur. This is where your work really makes a difference.

What, in your opinion, should a cartoonist aspire to above all else?

Aspire to make a difference! Make a difference in your town, in your state, in your country, in your world! Do something that's worthy of consideration. Cartoonists were not granted their powers to sit around and make safe, lazy "Bill Clinton got a blow-job" jokes!

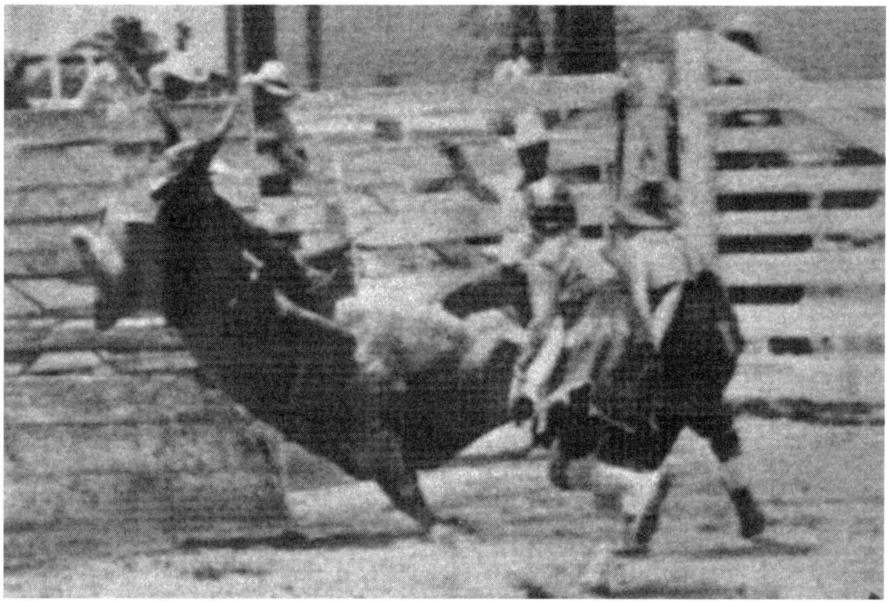

Sharpnack riding a bull at the Boulder County Fairgrounds in Colorado, 1978.

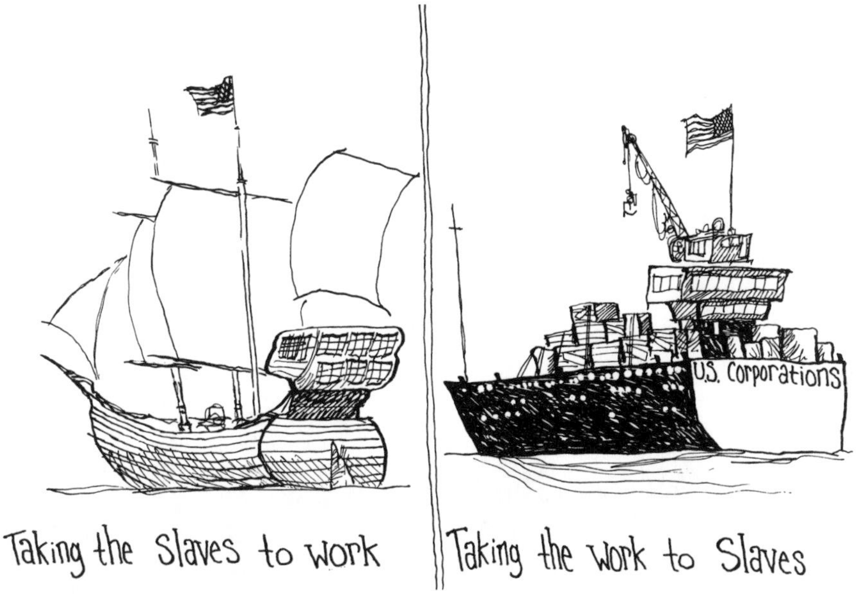
U.S. Corporations
Taking the Slaves to work
Taking the work to Slaves

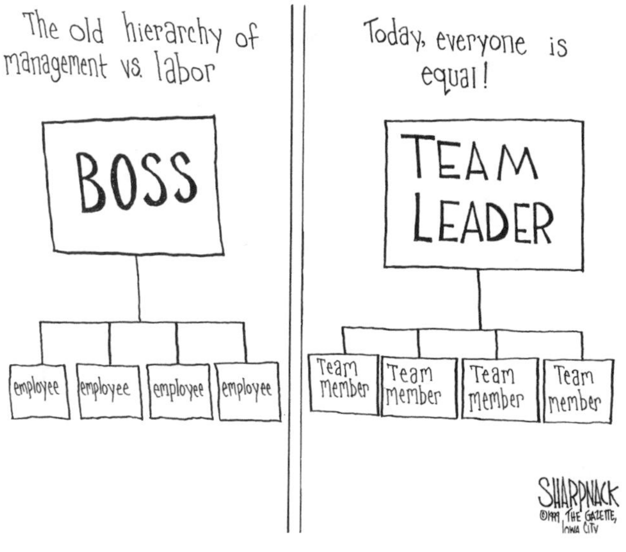
The old hierarchy of management vs. labor
BOSS
employee
employee
employee
employee
Today, everyone is equal!
TEAM LEADER
Team Member
Team Member
Team Member
Team Member
SHARPNACK ©1999 THE GAZETTE, Iowa City

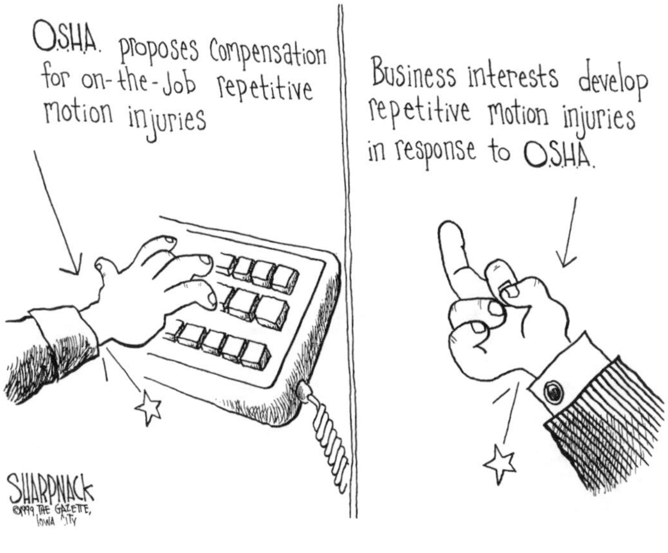
O.S.H.A. proposes Compensation for on-the-Job repetitive motion injuries
Business interests develop repetitive motion injuries in response to O.S.H.A.
SHARPNACK ©1999 THE GAZETTE, Iowa City

Cartoonists have an obligation to the world they live in!

What's this about an overdose? Of what? What happened?

I did mention that I made my living as a musician for many years, yes? It is a culture unto its own and dope usin' is a major part of it. In fact, half the bands I've ever been involved with may have just as well have had an application form requiring that you partake, on a regular basis, of a host of mind altering substances just to get hired.

In one particular band we decided that our drug of the week was the "black beauty," a substance that I had become familiar with working in gas fields which gave the user that "little extra kick" to make it through a 14-hour shift. Well, a drummer doesn't need that much of a kick and I took what I remembered as the "standard dose." Yow! I thought I was having a heart-attack and so did the rest of the band. Our bass player drove me to the ER where the attending staff pumped me full of sedatives and told me to "lay off the caffeine for awhile." I paid them in cash.

Let's face it: We're not an especially qualified group of people when it comes to spewing opinions on a variety of topics. Why the hell should anyone care what we think about the Middle East, global warming and the tax code?

Who's "qualified" to spew opinions on any subject? We're as "qualified" as anybody. In fact, we're more "qualified" than most media outlets. We pay attention. We analyze. We're doing the work that the "news media" has decided not to do (oh, gee! someone might not like us if we run a real story). Be it merely our opinion, we're still probably the best source of what's actually happening.

What do you wish you did better as a cartoonist, and what do you think you do exceedingly well?

I wish I was a better caricaturist. The good ones can make a fortune at county fair midways! It takes me a month to get a new face down. But, hey, that's what labels are for!

What I think I do exceptionally well is render expressions on the faces of my subjects. By using just two little dots for eyes, positioned in the perfect spot, you can tell what the character is thinking or feeling.

NOW SERVING OVER 6,000,000,000 (while Supplies last)

Groupie memorabilia.

Eric Bezdek

His "Corn Valley" analyzes a uniquely American state of mind

Eric Bezdek, 32, is a relatively new voice in the world of alternative political cartooning. Like Don Asmussen, most of his work is locally-oriented. His strip "Corn Valley" is based at the *Eugene Comic News* in Oregon, though his missives on pollution and other environmental concerns also appear in *Funny Times* and *Z* magazine. A staffer at Portland's *Bear Deluxe* magazine, Bezdek is also a freelance illustrator as well as a teacher at an alternative school in Oregon.

What's the conceit of "Corn Valley"? Why the name?

Corn Valley is short for Corvallis, Oregon, where I lived when I started regularly drawing cartoons. I adopted the name because it sounded funny, both idealistic and disgusting. It reminded me of "Bloom County." It's a tribute to that general area of the Willamette Valley where I used to live. It's really meaningless; it's glib.

Are there any other working cartoonists who mine the same terrain as you do in "Corn Valley"?

Sure. Editorial cartoons seems to me to offer both the biggest market and the best opportunities for publication for an independent cartoonist.

The funny pages are locked up by the newspaper syndicates but the editorial page offers some opportunities.

The detail work that you do makes clear that your drawing style is a deliberate decision to explore abstraction and looseness at the expense of tightness. Why do you choose to render your work in a way that might make some readers think it's amateurish?

Eric assists his niece, Raven, with a pressing problem.

Hmm ... Not sure what you mean by amateurish. I use paper, quill pens, and brushes to draw my cartoons and I guess by some standards my process might be considered amateur. I enjoy it. In general I have worked to simplify and clean up my drawing style, to make it reproduce better on newsprint. I like abstraction; my favorite paintings are by cubist painters. In the book *Understanding Comics* by Scott McCloud there is a great explanation of drawing styles and how they relate to the comics reader. He says something like highly-detailed drawing tends to make the reader perceive the character as a specific person, whereas more simplified drawings tend to be perceived as anyone.

Something you have in common with other participants in this book, such as Andy Singer, is your obvious dislike for car culture, as epitomized by traffic jams and road rage. Where do you live that traffic is such a problem?

I really enjoy Andy Singer's cartoons. I think he lives in Minnesota [actually, he lives in California]... don't know what the traffic is like there. I lived in Portland, Oregon when I drew some of my car-relat-

Eric Bezdek

ed cartoons. The traffic is horrible there. All the freeways lead right into the center of town. There is no good way around it. Once I was stuck in traffic and I saw two guys in front of me get out of their cars and start fist-fighting right in the middle of the freeway. It was the best thing ever! I watched for a minute but then traffic started moving so I drove around them. It was good to get ahead a couple of cars.

Your cartoons are characterized by the anti-punch line. Not only is there no punch line, you seem to wallow in ambiguity and an unwillingness to resolve issues posed within a cartoon. Are you trying to make a point using this device?

Ummm...Not really.

I seem to detect a vague "Bloom County" influence in your work. Am I correct?

Who else influenced you as a cartoonist?

I read "Bloom County" religiously as a kid, "Peanuts," "Calvin and Hobbes," and "The Far Side." I still get out the old books and read them sometimes before bed. It's really too bad to see Calvin urinating on the backs of so many trucks these days. Nowadays, I read Matt Groening, Ruben Bolling, Tom Tomorrow, Lloyd Dangle, Matt Wuerker, George Herriman and Robert Crumb.

You're a young guy, just starting out in the depressing world of alternative cartooning. Where do you see yourself in 10 years? 20?

Would you believe it if I said I have no idea? I never planned on having anything work out for me, but strangely enough some things have. I'm hoping for the best.

Who was your greatest positive influence on a personal level?

Not counting my parents or immediate family ... John Micheals. Calculus teacher at a community college I attended. He was a really genuine guy. He came to every class with a pot of really strong black coffee and a second pot of tea and began the class by offering everybody a cup of whichever they preferred. Then when we were awake he would find the person who least understood what was going on and then go through one problem on the board with them. Sometimes it took the whole class period to do just one, but it was great because by the time you left everyone understood that one problem.

In most classes I had ever been to before, we covered 10 to 20 problems and when I left my head was just spinning. If you didn't understand, it was your tough luck. And I was a really bad math student. Every time I opened the book it just put me to sleep, literally, right on the desk.

John made sure everyone got it before moving on. He actually cared that we learned something and we had a great time even if it meant we didn't cover everything. I became one of the better students in his class and I gained a lot of confidence in my abilities. I learned the process of problem-solving and that I could do math if I really put the effort into it. I just had never really been interested in it before. Once I realized that, I quit math and began taking drawing classes instead because art was what I had always enjoyed most.

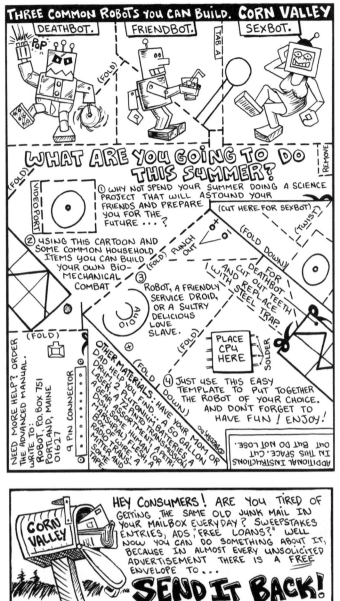

What kind of name is "Bezdek," ethnically? Just curious.

Czech.

When you were a kid, did you collect anything? What?

Nothing of value really. Have you ever read Shel Silverstein's *Hector the Collector*? I have a short attention span so my collections never amounted to much. I would collect a few of something and then move on to something else. I had a little bit of everything. A lot of stuff like you might find in a Cracker Jack box. Little toys that were small enough to fit in my pocket. Marbles, jacks, lenses, prisms, compasses, wire, nuts and bolts, pocket knives, rabbits' feet, inner tube patch kits, bottle caps, rocks, matchbooks... I would carry stuff in my pocket for awhile and then when it got too full I would take something out and put it in a box or on a shelf.

I have a bag of rubber bands from my newspaper route as a kid. On my newspaper route you had to roll the papers yourself and rubber-band them before you delivered them. When I started the route they gave me a massive bag of red rubber bands, maybe five or ten pounds. I have been trying to use them up ever since. I'm down to a sandwich bag full. Amazingly, they are still very supple and rubbery. I collect T-shirts. I would be glad to trade with any one who wants to. I also have a

pretty good tool collection going but that was gathered over the last 10 years or so as an adult.

Name your five favorite bands and tell me why they don't suck.

I really like the Squirrel Nut Zippers. I think I can dance to them.

If you had to lose a sense, which one would you go without?

Hearing.

Back to childhood: When kids were picked for teams, were you picked first, last or somewhere in between?

I was usually picked second or third.

What, in your opinion, should be the goal of every cartoonist?

Gobs and gobs of Green Cash Money.

> "I use paper, quill pens, and brushes to draw my cartoons and I guess by some standards my process might be considered amateurish. I enjoy it."

Everybody's got to have a hobby: two of Eric's T-shirts from his extensive collection.

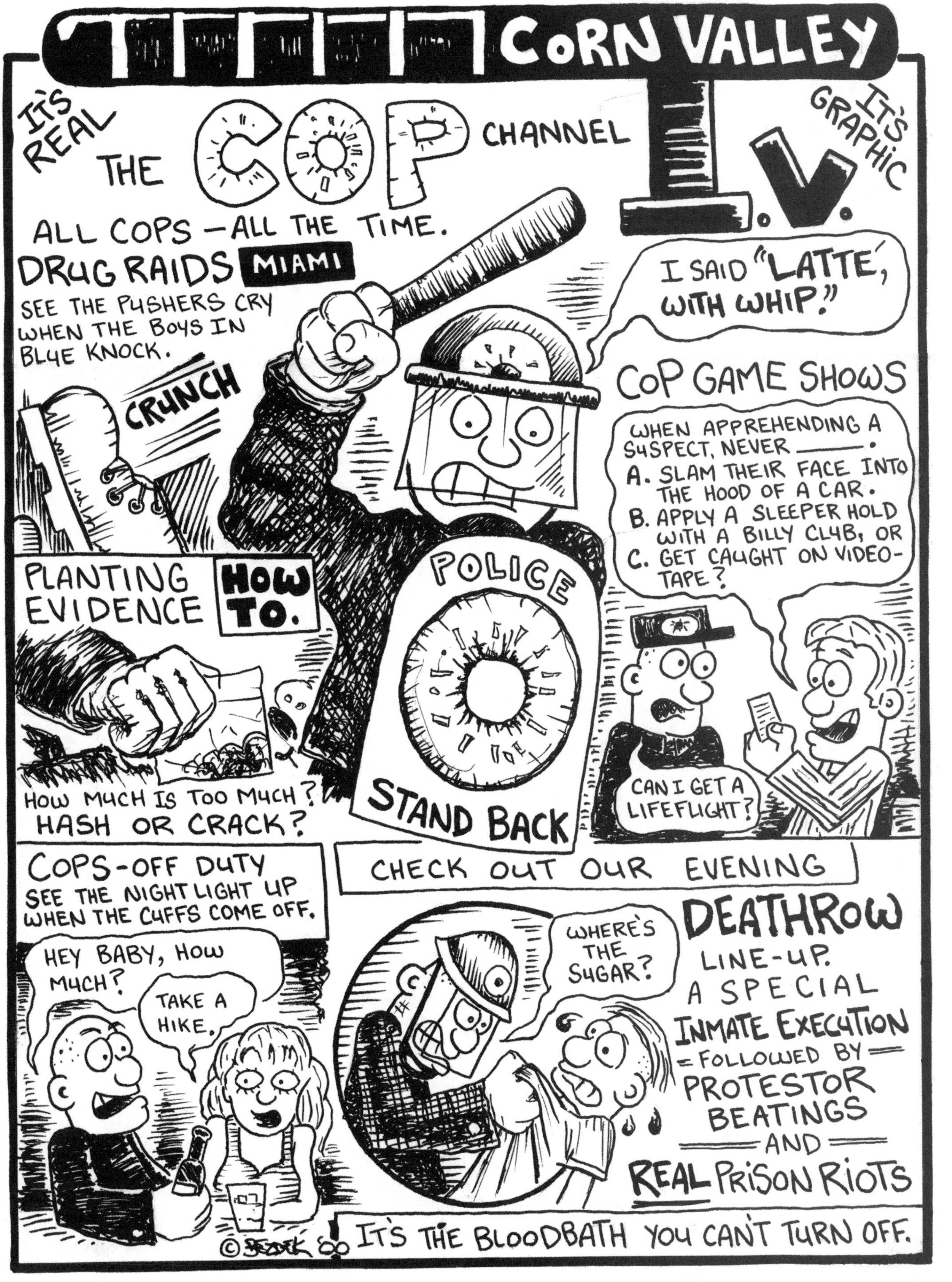
CORN VALLEY T.V.
IT'S REAL
THE COP CHANNEL
IT'S GRAPHIC
ALL COPS — ALL THE TIME.
DRUG RAIDS MIAMI
SEE THE PUSHERS CRY WHEN THE BOYS IN BLUE KNOCK.
CRUNCH
I SAID "LATTE, WITH WHIP."
COP GAME SHOWS
WHEN APPREHENDING A SUSPECT, NEVER ____.
A. SLAM THEIR FACE INTO THE HOOD OF A CAR.
B. APPLY A SLEEPER HOLD WITH A BILLY CLUB, OR
C. GET CAUGHT ON VIDEO-TAPE?
PLANTING EVIDENCE HOW TO.
POLICE
STAND BACK
CAN I GET A LIFEFLIGHT?
HOW MUCH IS TOO MUCH? HASH OR CRACK?
COPS-OFF DUTY
SEE THE NIGHT LIGHT UP WHEN THE CUFFS COME OFF.
CHECK OUT OUR EVENING
HEY BABY, HOW MUCH?
TAKE A HIKE.
WHERE'S THE SUGAR?
DEATHROW LINE-UP. A SPECIAL INMATE EXECUTION FOLLOWED BY PROTESTOR BEATINGS AND REAL PRISON RIOTS
IT'S THE BLOODBATH YOU CAN'T TURN OFF.
© BEZDEK '00

Ruben Bolling

"Tom the Dancing Bug" may—or may not—be the most brilliant comic strip ever

"Tom the Dancing Bug," a weekly strip syndicated by Universal Press Syndicate, is the only cartoon feature that I will admit is better than mine. New Yorker Ruben Bolling, 39, debuted, as I did, in *NY Perspectives* during the early '90's. His work now appears in more than 60 publications, including the *Village Voice, SF Weekly, New York Times* and *Washington Post.* A Wall Street investment banker and Harvard Law School graduate, Bolling applies his intelligence and adult experience to a sensibility straight out of junior high school to produce sublime sociopolitical commentary.

TED RALL: I'm only asking this question because I already know that in your case the answer is interesting: How did you first get into cartooning? (Hint: Tell us about the evil dean.)

RUBEN BOLLING: While attending law school, I saw an ad in the school newspaper saying they needed a cartoonist. I developed a comic strip in about an hour—inventing essentially the exact format I still use today, 15 years later—and submitted it as a weekly strip that would have no title. The editor accepted the strip, but in-sisted on a title. Out of spite, I gave him the stupidest name I could think of: "Tom the Dancing Bug." Of course, on my way home, I realized that the name was perfect.

I also wanted a pseudonym, mostly because I simply didn't want classmates to know I was the cartoonist, but probably also for psychological reasons too complex for me to fathom.

After my third comic was published, a comic attacking a particularly vindictive dean, I found another reason a pseudonym came in handy: I was told that the dean

Young Ruben Bolling. Note the primordial cartoon in the foreground.

was trying to find out who this "Ruben Bolling" was. After that, the pseudonym was kept a secret.

I have to say that I was terribly disappointed the first time I met you. Here you were, the creator of this incredibly original and hilarious comic strip, and you were the straightest guy in the world: Short hair, corporate job, even stiffer than me! You were wearing a suit! Do you ever have the urge to burst out, grab a backpack and some Birkenstocks and go hitchhiking through Tibet?

I know, I remember that meeting. You, on the other hand, did not disappoint at all. With flowing Jesus-like hair, wearing nothing but a Speedo bathing suit, you entered the restaurant and within minutes had regaled all the diners with hilarious anecdotes, convinced a bickering couple to get married, and organized the wait staff into a union. I don't wear a suit anymore.

Your cartoons require a unique combination of pop culture knowledge and highbrow exposure to anthropology and

other sciences to fully appreciate. Who is the typical "Tom the Dancing Bug" fan?

I don't think it's quite as narrow as that. It's relatively rare that I'll include a truly esoteric reference and when I do, I try to make sure that it can be appreciated on some other level. I guess the bottom line is that I never talk down to my audience; I try to write for myself (to a reasonable degree; I don't include jokes about my sister-in-law).

More than most cartoonists, you revisit sub-comic strips within your work from time to time. "The Education of Louis" deals with the trials and tribulations of a perfectly ordinary suburban kid. "Super Fun-Pak Comics" collects satirical take-offs of the comic strip genre. Even "The Impossible Squad," a blood-and-guts comics take-off, made a reappearance. Do readers ever complain that you're recycling old ideas?

I can't begin to tell you how much the opposite is true. Most of my mail is from readers asking for more of one format/character or another. But, come on, the exploration of recurring characters and themes is not "recycling old ideas"; it's a hugely important part of cartooning. Coming up with a new, interesting God-Man adventure, for example, is about as invigorating and creatively challenging as any aspect of producing "Tom the Dancing Bug."

Of course, the key is making sure the new adventure is in fact new and interesting—the danger is that you end up beating something into the ground. I go by instinct; when I get bored of a character, that's a good sign that it's time to let it go. I've "retired" a number of characters (I still get mail requesting more "Harvey Richards, Lawyer for Children," and I've used him only once in the past five or so years), and replaced them with new ones. That ensures that the strip stays fresh and interesting for me (and hopefully the readers).

You've developed a highly competent drawing style that allows you to simultaneously do highly abstract and highly realistic characters within the same panel. Do you use a dead line—one that doesn't vary in thickness—intentionally to achieve this effect? To whom do you owe your artistic influences?

I use a dead line because I'm not nearly proficient enough to employ brush work. I use a Rapidograph and do the best I can to achieve whatever style I'm aiming for in a given comic. I'm not trained in art at all, so I've worked hard to use my limited tools and abilities to fake it.

The fact that I change styles depending on the idea keeps the process of drawing very interesting to me. For example, when I'm drawing a God-Man comic, I use a super-hero comic book style, and I have a lot of fun evoking Curt Swan, or Gil Kane or Will Eisner or Jack Kirby in any panel. With Super-Fun-Pak Comix, I can borrow styles from any of the daily comics page guys, and that's a blast too. With Billy Dare (and before him, "Sam Roland, the Detective Who Dies"), I was sort of going for a Herge/Tintin look.

But when I'm not consciously trying to conjure up an artist's or genre's style, I'd say my biggest artistic influences were the Mad comic book guys, particularly Bill Elder and Wally Wood. Not that my art even approaches their level, but that's what I often aim for. I think those first 23 issues of *Mad* were the best humor cartooning ever done.

> "I was told the dean was trying to find out who this "Ruben Bolling" was. After that, the pseudonym was kept a secret."

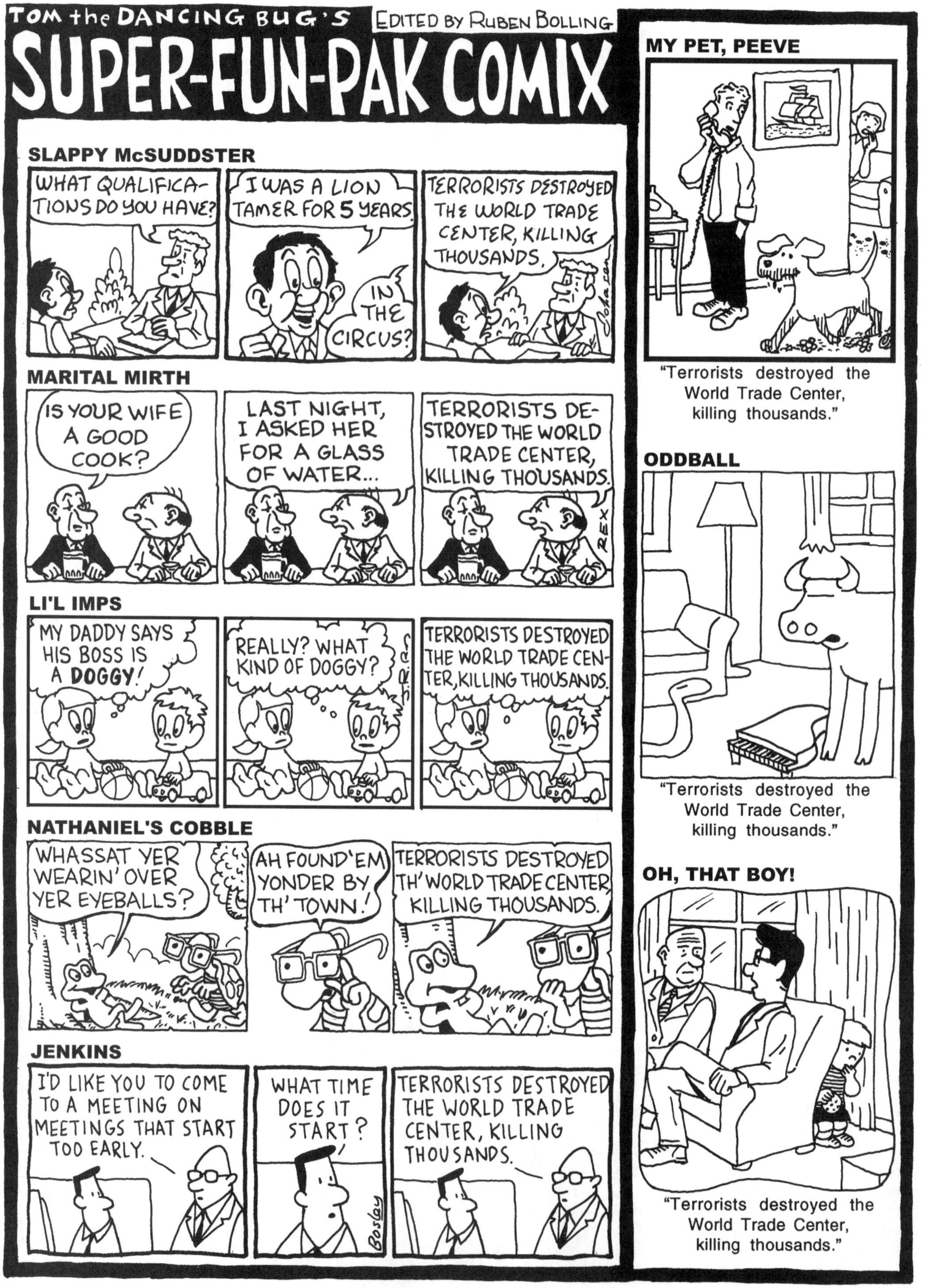
TOM the DANCING BUG'S
EDITED BY RUBEN BOLLING
SUPER-FUN-PAK COMIX
SLAPPY McSUDDSTER
WHAT QUALIFICATIONS DO YOU HAVE?
I WAS A LION TAMER FOR 5 YEARS.
IN THE CIRCUS?
TERRORISTS DESTROYED THE WORLD TRADE CENTER, KILLING THOUSANDS.
MARITAL MIRTH
IS YOUR WIFE A GOOD COOK?
LAST NIGHT, I ASKED HER FOR A GLASS OF WATER...
TERRORISTS DESTROYED THE WORLD TRADE CENTER, KILLING THOUSANDS.
REX
LI'L IMPS
MY DADDY SAYS HIS BOSS IS A DOGGY!
REALLY? WHAT KIND OF DOGGY?
TERRORISTS DESTROYED THE WORLD TRADE CENTER, KILLING THOUSANDS.
NATHANIEL'S COBBLE
WHASSAT YER WEARIN' OVER YER EYEBALLS?
AH FOUND 'EM YONDER BY TH' TOWN!
TERRORISTS DESTROYED TH' WORLD TRADE CENTER, KILLING THOUSANDS.
JENKINS
I'D LIKE YOU TO COME TO A MEETING ON MEETINGS THAT START TOO EARLY.
WHAT TIME DOES IT START?
TERRORISTS DESTROYED THE WORLD TRADE CENTER, KILLING THOUSANDS.
MY PET, PEEVE
"Terrorists destroyed the World Trade Center, killing thousands."
ODDBALL
"Terrorists destroyed the World Trade Center, killing thousands."
OH, THAT BOY!
"Terrorists destroyed the World Trade Center, killing thousands."

For the hippest cartoonist in the biz, you like truly crappy classic-rock music—Steely Dan, Bruce Springsteen. Shouldn't the genius behind "Tom the Dancing Bug" draw to the hip, intelligent sounds of J Church, the Mr. T Experience and Stereolab?

Yes.

How does your background as a lawyer—albeit a non-practicing one—affect your work?

I think I'm drawn to issues, and the logical inconsistencies of ideological positions, more than most cartoonists. I don't get as involved in politics (power plays, personalities, etc.) as other cartoonists who do topical stuff.

Would you buy two $500 suits or one $1,000 suit?

I don't wear suits anymore. I now only wear Speedo bathing suits.

Describe the process that leads from the germ of an idea to a final cartoon.

For some comics, the whole comic comes to me all at once and I just write words as fast as I can because I'm basically transcribing, not writing. For other comics, I'll get some thought that interests me and I'll write it down and think

about it, turning it over in my mind, until I realize where the comic is.

Who is the worst editor in America and why?

There are no bad editors, only editors who make poor choices.

Does it feel strange to appear in high-falutin' venues like *The New Yorker* and *The New York Times*?

It does. When I was first in *The New Yorker*, my mother told me that my grandfather loved the magazine and read it every week, and it made me very

proud that I became part of that institution. But I'm honestly most proud of, and most grateful for, the newspapers that run "Tom" every week—that the editors set aside the space for me to become a part of the weekly routine of their readers.

Sometimes it seems that with your political work you're trying to summon up a rage that may or may not be there. Do you ever find that you're intellectually annoyed by a politician or a phenomenon without feeling the requisite visceral anger to go along with it?

> "I look at my political stuff as an opportunity to point out a flaw in an argument in an ongoing debate, or laugh at the absurdity of the process."

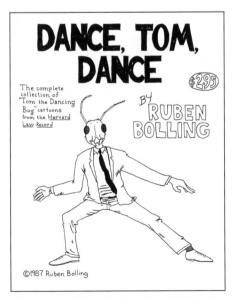

The cover of Bolling's self-published compilation of his school comic strip, xeroxed and sold in the school bookstore. Bolling calls it his only publishing venture that was an unqualified success.

I don't think I ever try to "summon up a rage," and I don't think "visceral anger" is a "requisite" part of cartooning. We just have very different approaches; I look at my political stuff as an opportunity to make fun of a position, point out a flaw in an argument in an ongoing national debate, or laugh at the absurdity of the process. Even when an issue really does make me angry, doing a comic on it is never an angry process for me.

Please describe for our humble gathering your philosophy about the 30-minute TV show limitation.

Um...I don't ever sit down with the intention of watching TV for more than 30 minutes, so I almost never watch hour-long shows.

Yes, but you freely admit to watching broadcast films, and baseball games, that last two hours or more. So why not watch hour-long programs? Admit it — this is one strange way to live your life.

This is one of the many enigmas that comprise the complex and richly textured man Ruben Bolling. Can we possibly hope to fathom the reasoning behind, or the meaning of, this puzzling practice? No, but if we do not try, haven't we given up on our own humanity? Perhaps.

What is the stupidest question I've asked you in this interview?

This last one.

William Brown

President Bill becomes plain old "Citizen Bill," but that's OK

"Citizen Bill," progeny of the late "President Bill," is the progeny of the twisted, detailed imagination of Washington-based William "Bill" Brown, a cartoonist who mourns the wasted potential of anarchic fun that could be had if only he were to become Supreme Leader of these United States. Brown, 50, publishes "Citizen Bill," his post-presidential rumination on the American zeitgeist, in the *Takoma Voice, Comic Relief* and *Funny Times;* it's hard to imagine where Brown's work would appear if not for the alternative press.

TED RALL: "President Bill" is a difficult strip to categorize. It's a what-if scenario, born of Reagan-Bushism and continued throughout the Clinton era, about a guy who becomes president by lottery, and the guy is probably you. Am I right?

BILL BROWN: Is President Bill me? Yes and no. The character is based on myself certainly, but the cartoon character is more of what some people might call a woolly-headed or knee-jerk liberal than I am. Generally, President Bill is me before reason prevails.

I would characterize "President Bill" (and to a lesser extent, "Citizen Bill") as a "concept cartoon" or maybe an "improv-

comic." I improvised on the news events of the day (for instance: the War on Drugs), reversing the politics (President Bill's War on Junk Food), combining them with the events of my life (my kids craving Pop Tarts) or the lives of my friends, and managed to spin a continuing story line from week to week.

As for the "concept" part—there really was a President Bill Administration which existed as a sort of shadow government: I appointed all my friends to cabinet and other government posts, only a few of which I made up (Department of Humor, for instance). A lot of my friends worked in typical low to middle-level Washington jobs and were the sort of people who defi-

nitely didn't get invited to the Washington parties that get written up in the *Post* Style section. I put that in the past tense because one of my good friends, whom I named Secretary of State is now rather prominent in the Foreign Service—yet another case of President Bill prescience. The main example of President Bill's prescience is the Clinton Administration.

The *Washington* (DC) *City Paper* was horrified when they found out I was using real people a few months after the feature had been running. Their lawyers made me get signatures on a release form from every person I depicted. The President Bill Library (two file drawers in my studio) contain all these forms, the letters of appointment and acceptance, correspondence with my appointees, reference materials, photos of the Inaugural Ball (held at Blobb's Park, a German beer hall near Baltimore) and so forth. Historians will find this a treasure trove and I'm a little puzzled why none have shown up yet.

Obviously, you've given a lot of thought to the presidency. What would you do during your first hundred days? And can a president really make much of a difference anymore?

This country has a habit of befriending, training, and arming unsavory foreign leaders like Manuel Noreiga, Sadam Hussein, and Osama bin Laden, only to find itself fighting them later.

Son, I want you to always keep this list of our new allies in the war against terrorism.

Why, Dad?

So you'll know who our enemies will be when you grow up.

Can a presidency make much of a difference? Try me!

Day One: the SUV Exchange Program—a purely volunteer exchange of SUVs for bicycles.

Day Two: Clean Air and Clear Highway Act: Anyone caught driving an SUV will be staked out on the roof of their vehicle by the side of the road and left to die.

Day Three: Operation Wet Arches: proclaim all McDonalds and other fast-food franchise sites to be wetlands, and have them flooded.

Day Four: The Musicians' Full Employment Act: ban use of recorded music in public places.

Day Five: Morris Dance Proclamation: schools to replace all sports and other physical education activities with Morris dance.

Day Six: Beer Day: to celebrate the Morris Dance Proclamation, all corporate breweries will be broken up into micro-breweries, and making beer with artificial carbonation will become a felony.

Day Seven: Place moratorium on prison-building, legalize drugs.

Day Eight: Make disobeying a parent a federal offense, establish legal drug-taking age at 30 and lift moratorium on prison-building.

If you got that phone call appointing you president, would you hang up or pack for 1600 Pennsylvania Avenue?

You have to admit that I would be an improvement over the current situation.

You use what some nimrods call a "woodcut" style, which I know from personal experience is really scratchboard. I stopped using the stuff after I found it increasingly difficult to find. Got a secret stash? Can I break into it?

You can get *anything* on eBay!

At some point "President Bill" became "Citizen Bill." When, why and what's up with that?

I couldn't get a lawyer to take my copyright-violation case against that imitation President Bill guy. Not only did he steal the name, he swiped most of the plot and the ideas—which he watered down considerably. He was a baby-boomer, draft-dodging, '60's anti-war type with a feminist wife, a child, and a (supposedly) liberal agenda. It was obvious after his election that not only would the "President Bill" name become confusing, the cartoon wouldn't be as funny with a Democrat in office. Not enough contrast.

Another important reason I changed was that publishers wouldn't do another "President Bill" book, despite the fact that after the first book the cartoon's satire became sharper and the artwork was much better. One publisher told me the newer material was "too dark," which I suspect meant it was too critical of the Gulf War for them. Someday, I hope that material gets published in book form.

I also was having problems making ends meet because the cartoon took so long to produce each week, a problem I've since eliminated thanks to technology which enables me to do the text portions of each panel on the computer rather than by hand, which was very time consuming (and not as legible).

Shortly after I ended "President Bill", I took Eric Bond, my local newspaper editor, up on his offer to continue the feature without the presidential trappings, and with local themes. It didn't take me very long to realize that "Citizen Bill" had wider-than-local appeal. The small-town, suburban, civic and social issues are common to many people across the country. That's why local names and places seldom appear in the feature.

More than anything else, your vision of the presidency seems to be exquisitely playful. Is that a reflection of your personality and would you like to see a president who seems to be having an anarchic, rip-roaring time in office? After all, JFK really loved the gig, and he's the last one any of us cared about.

Of course JFK loved the gig—he had hot- and cold-running women, drugs, liquor, and no press scrutiny. I, of course, would never betray the public's trust in this manner.

It's prediction time. By what years would you expect to see the first African-American, female or non-Christian presidents?

I think we'll start seeing female, African-American, Asian and other minority-group candidates as a standard campaign feature by 2008, if not 2004. I suspect we'll have an Hispanic president before we have an African-American one. I'd guess that'll happen around 2012 or 2018. He or she will be a Republican.

The Brown clan, the inspiration for many a "Citizen Bill" rant.

Describe your ideal Saturday.

Well, if I can't get a zeppelin ride over the Alps, I'll take the usual: doing something active with my family and friends. This would usually involve Morris dancing, singing and drinking good beer.

If you had to live in a country other than the US, where would you go for your exile?

England—for the beer and Morris dancing.

What single problem should the US work to resolve first?

We should focus all our attention and our resources on the Beer Gap between the US and just about every other nation in the world. We have the highest standard of living yet the worst beer on the planet. Real beer does not have carbon dioxide in it.

What's your take on affirmative action?

It is a pernicious form of reverse discrimination and the instant that we have achieved racial equality we should discontinue it.

I can't figure it out, so I'll just ask: are you an incredibly joyful, or incredibly pissed-off individual?

I have to admit I am incredibly pissed-off, especially when I see the things people do, particularly when it comes to global warming. Stupid political policies can usually be reversed but stupid environmental choices can't. Channeling my anger into humor keeps me sane and easier to live with (not that I'm easy to live with as it is).

The US seems to have suffered from a distinct lack of ideological competition since the demise of the Soviet Union. Were we better off with an enemy, albeit a phony one?

The Left is best rid of the embarrassment of Soviet-style communism. However, it should continue to be deeply ashamed of itself for ever defending it. I hope it learns the lesson—but I doubt it.

What's the worst habit you have?

I'll have to refer you to my wife and children on that one.

Who are your primary artistic influences?

William Morris, who founded the Arts and Crafts Movement in the mid-19th century, and John Held, Jr., American cartoonist of the '20's.

What's the most attractive American city? The least?

I haven't traveled extensively in the US, especially since I started having children, but the most attractive US city I've been to is San Francisco. I have to say the least attractive is Washington, DC. Outside of the small federal/monumental areas it has very little architectural or geographical character. Also, it is miserably hot and unbearably humid in the summer.

What are you reading right now?

You've caught me at the one time in the year—summer vacation—when I find time to read, and I tend to read everything at once, jumping from book to book. So, unlike the rest of the year when it takes me months to finish one book, I'm currently reading five books:

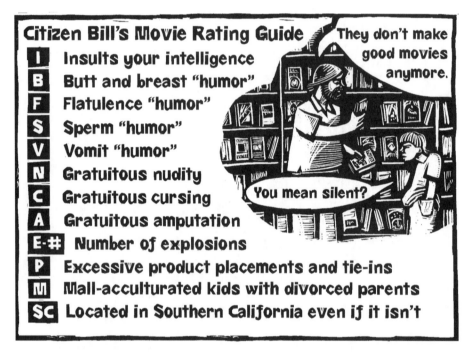

Positively 4th Street, by David Hajdu, *Fast Food Nation* by Eric Schlosser, *The White Man in the Tree and other stories* by Mark Kurlansky, *The Direction of Play* by Takeo Kajiwara (a book on the game of Go), and *Bayou Farewell* by Mike Tidwell (unpublished—he's letting me read the manuscript).

Which movie have you seen the most times?

Citizen Kane, but that wasn't by choice. I was forced to watch it repeatedly for a college course. After that it's hard to say which I've seen the most times: *Casablanca, The Russians Are Coming, The Russians Are Coming, Kind Hearts and Coronets, The General*, or (thanks to late-night TV movies) *Mad Max*.

What's your strangest interaction with a reader?

I can't say any have been strange. I've had lots of positive experiences meeting readers in person or getting letters from them. It's great to have a cartoon that originates in my local paper—I get friendly greetings on the street (and lots of ideas suggested for cartoons, some of them useful). These interactions make me realize that in some ways I'm providing a public service, expressing views that many people hold but don't have the resources to voice.

I've also learned to be a little careful about who I make fun of. Elected politicians are fair game, but city employees are another matter. I did a cartoon that depicted a police officer talking to a city resident. The target of my humor was the resident, but the police department made it plain in a couple of letters that they took it the wrong way. I failed to consider that city workers, even police officers, are employees of us residents, and it is grossly unfair for employers to publicly ridicule employees, even if the ridicule is not intended, just perceived.

One interaction that always haunts me is when my "President Bill" book publisher told me that someone called saying they were with a movie company (though they wouldn't say which one), and they were interested in making a movie out of the book. The publisher said the person calling lost interest when the publisher told them to speak to my agent, not me. They never called the agent. About a year later the movie "Dave" came out, which has a similar theme about a "regular" guy becoming president, though the plot and the politics are completely different from "President Bill." I have to wonder about that.

Ward Sutton

The alternative press' most gifted caricaturist turns his sights on politics and culture

Ward Sutton is a brilliant magazine illustrator (for *The New York Times Magazine, Entertainment Weekly* and countless other publications) who in 1995 decided to start a weekly comic about music. Soon his strip "Schlock 'N' Roll," was picked up by *The Village Voice* in 1998, began tackling pop culture, then social issues and ultimately politics and current events. While most alternative artists work in more abstract forms, the 35-year-old Sutton's work has graced the covers of *Rolling Stone* and *TV Guide.*

TED RALL: You were already a successful illustrator before you began drawing "Schlock 'N' Roll." Why did you decide to make the move to the comparatively low-paying field of weekly strip cartooning?

WARD SUTTON: Actually, my career history is a bit more complicated. I graduated from college in 1989 and moved to Minneapolis and tried to find work doing about anything related to cartoons or illustration. I had some good fortune and a year later the local *Twin Cities Reader* hired me to do a weekly cartoon for them. I had only been doing it for a year when I decided to move to Seattle. The Reader let me continue the strip, "Ward's Cleaver," for them—and I did—throughout my four

Sutton in 1990, in a local TV station interview. His hair is now substantially shorter.

years in Seattle and my first two in New York. It wasn't easy—as editors at the *Reader* changed, their concept of the strip changed, and sometimes I was forced to comment on Minneapolis current events even though I didn't actually live in Minneapolis.

During my Seattle years, I was also doing illustration. I was having some success but eventually hit a ceiling for what I could accomplish there. That helped prompt the move to NYC in 1995. Then, just as I left Seattle, the local music paper, *The Rocket,* asked me to start a regular comic strip for them. Now I was going to be doing two different comic strips that ran in towns I didn't live in!

I got to New York and hit the ground running in terms of my illustration career, but the cartoons were my labor of love and I tried hard to find a paper that would run them locally. At this point, I was becoming frustrated with the format and constraints on "Ward's Cleaver." I felt my other strip, "Schlock 'N' Roll" was my punk rock cartoon, where I could just do anything at all. I even drew it (in the beginning) in a less-refined, spontaneous scribble style.

Correct me if I'm wrong, but it seems that "S&R" began as more of a commentary about such pop cultural phenomena as

MTV, fashion models and reality TV. While you still mine that territory, you've branched out to political and social commentary. How come?

When I first started "S&R" it was actually only about music. Back then, I did the strip biweekly because that was how often *The Rocket* came out. When the *Voice* picked it up, I started doing it weekly and it was pretty hard to think up something to comment on in the music realm every week. Plus, rock 'n' roll was changing as were my feelings about it. When I started the strip I really wanted to vent my soul about all the things that were ridiculous in the rock world (having worked in record stores and lived in Seattle in the early '90's, I had plenty of fodder!), but eventually I just cared a lot less about modern music than I did in the beginning. I decided to broaden the scope to cover all aspects of culture, including politics. But I do think at this point the fact that I often comment on pop culture is one of the things that makes my strip unique.

You may be the most earnest working political cartoonist in America—sort of a Mister Smith Goes to Washington Meets VH1 in the West Village. (Does that mean anything?) Anyway: Are you really, truly surprised when elected officials abuse their power and ignore their constituents or are you really just as cynical and hard-hearted as the rest of us?

Your question actually surprises me because I feel like I am incredibly cynical. But I guess I do have an optimism that hopefully comes out in my work in one way or another. I think the event that really broke my naive idealism was the Gulf War. I truly was surprised by that... shocked that it could happen. Seeing George Bush Sr. out on the golf course in the summer of 1990 refusing to let Saddam Hussein's invasion of Kuwait interrupt his vacation, the subsequent hype and sense of inevitability about America's involvement, the jingoistic attitudes, the public apathy, the blind coverage by the media, the endless, self-congratulatory post-war parades... it all soured me pretty good. In fact, I think that war gave me a real sense of mission in my cartooning that I still feel.

If you could choose between doing

just illustrations and just "Schlock 'N' Roll," which would you choose?

If I could choose, I would choose not to choose—in other words, I would continue doing both. But if I had to choose, I would choose "S&R," unless pragmatic concerns (i.e. money) forced me to do otherwise. I enjoy illustration but at this point I am really more interested in creating the image and the idea. I made a conscious decision in 1999 to start turning down illustration work and focus more on cartooning. It was at that point that I started doing freelance cartoons for the *New York Times, Entertainment Weekly, Rolling Stone,* etc, and created my bi-weekly strip ("That's Entertoonment") for *TV Guide,* as well as making more of an effort to get "Schlock 'N' Roll" more widely syndicated.

Does violence ever have a place in the quest for political change, and if so when and how?

I guess I'd fall closer to Gandhi than the Weathermen on this question, but I don't think I could give an absolute answer. If we could go back in time and kill Hitler as a baby knowing what we know now, would we? Seems to me that would be the moral thing to do. But it's a slippery slope—there are a lot of wackos out there who THINK they're operating justly and they are really just a bigger problem themselves. Timothy McVeigh, for instance, seemed to think he was

Ward Sutton addresses fellow Gulf War protesters shutting down the Federal Building in Minneapolis, January, 1991.

doing what was best for his "cause." If you believe violence has a place then it's all up to what crusade someone chooses... so I am against the use of violence in general while I hold the wishy-washy caveat that it is sometimes necessary.

What would you personally be willing to sacrifice to see our society become a better place?

Let's see, I would sacrifice my dangerous, gas-guzzling SUV; my gun collection and membership to the NRA; my noise-, air-, and water-polluting speed boat; my trips to soulless discount chain warehouse stores; my meals at fast food restaurants; my air conditioner; my micro-wave oven; my insistence on getting a plastic bag to carry every already-overly-prewrapped-in plastic piece of consumer trash that I buy; my Prozac; my cigarettes; my overly-processed convenience food at supermarkets; any plans of shipping off future children to some sterile, life-draining day care so my wife and I can work a zillion hours a week in order to buy more things we will never use; my novelty T-shirts with "hilarious" lewd phrases on them; my piss-water beer, like Budweiser; my daily lotto tickets; my hours spent sitting in front of the TV; my attendance at WWF "smack-downs"; my participation in pro-life harassment of abortion clinics; my love of littering; my regular attendance at strip clubs; my purchasing tons of "disposable" products instead of reusable ones; my unending consumption of absolutely nutrient-free soda pop; my trips to casinos; my refusal to pay higher taxes in order to improve schools; my belief that what our city really needs is a new stadium; my goose-stepping on the consumer treadmill behind the latest trends in professional sports, brainless Hollywood blockbusters, formulaic TV shows, painfully bland and/or offensively bad pop music; that warm, self-congratulatory feeling I get when I buy a product boasting some obviously hollow claim that it is "good for the environment!" "fat free!" or simply "lite;" my jet-ski; my rider mower; my landfill; my nuclear power plant; my arsenal of weapons of mass destruction; and my current president of the United States.

Please describe the worst date and/or sexual experience of your life.

The date occurred when I was in high school. I asked this girl to a movie out of the blue and I didn't know her much at all. First, I wore a sweater because I thought it would look "nice"... but it was hot out and I sweated like a pig the whole night. Then, I was a half hour late to pick her up because I couldn't find her house. Then, because I was so late, we couldn't get tickets to the movie we wanted to see and were forced to see the only other option, a Disney-esque kids movie, "The Golden Seal" (about a lost seal who finds his way home, yadda, yadda, yadda). Then, the movie was so packed we couldn't get seats together in the theater. Then, after we left, I asked if she would like to get dinner or ice cream. She said no. We went to a diner anyway. I ate and she sipped on a Diet Coke. A guy from my high school was working there as a busboy and kept looking at us funny. Then— no joke—the homecoming king and queen from our school came in and sat in the booth right next to ours. Behind my date's back they openly mocked me/us making kissy faces, lewd gestures, etc. I promptly drove her home — no chance of anything close to a goodnight kiss, obviously. It was all over before 10 pm... I drove over to a hamburger place a friend of mine worked at and relayed the tale of the humiliating night, feeling like a total geek. (I actually did a cartoon about this once for a publication geared towards high school kids.)

All cartoonists receive letters from aspiring cartoonists. What do you tell people who ask for advice for breaking into the profession?

I just try to be both honest and supportive. I saw a documentary about Al Hirschfeld and he said he tries to discourage young cartoonists because you can't make a living at it these days. What a load of bullshit. I love Hirschfeld's work, but with that attitude we'd all be cogs stuffed in cubicles in some monolithic corporate headquarters somewhere.

Do you think it's possible for a politician to work within the system for years, yet remain pure and uncorrupted by corporations and other special interests?

Working within the system these days means getting in bed with corporations and special interests. And under this current system I believe one has to make it in to get anything done. But I think one can do so and still fight for what's right, even if it is tempered or somewhat compromised.

America seems adrift spiritually, culturally and politically. Do you agree with that assumption? If so, is it good or bad for political cartooning?

I don't know if adrift is the right word... segmented, maybe? With some of the segments being adrift? I do think we are going through continued cultural change, even if it doesn't seem as dramatic as something like the '60's did. It is good for cartooning but possibly bad for cartoonists who create simplistic cartoons. I think it is a good time for alternative cartoonists who don't try to sum up an event or phenomenon in a one-panel gag.

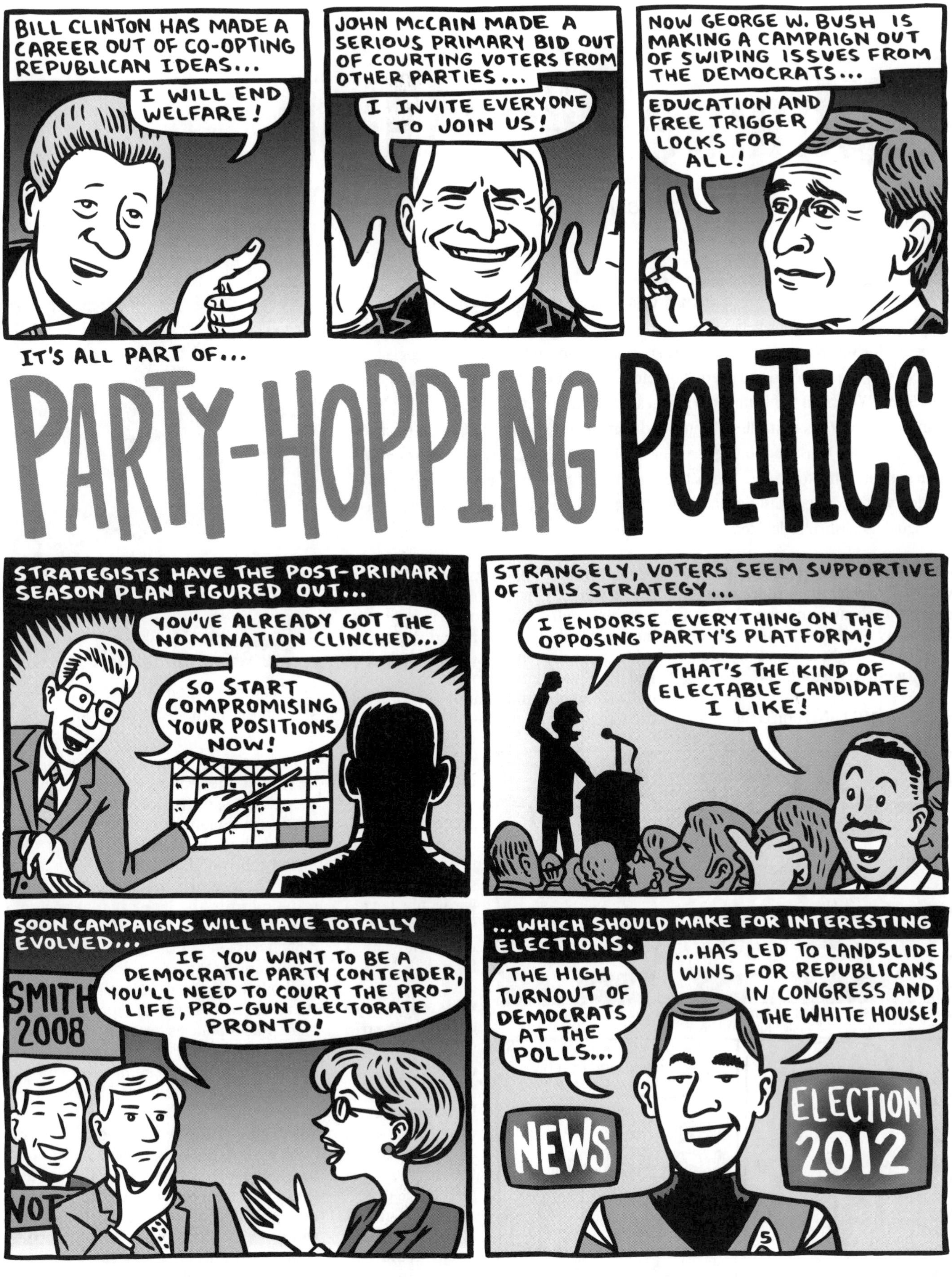
BILL CLINTON HAS MADE A CAREER OUT OF CO-OPTING REPUBLICAN IDEAS...
I WILL END WELFARE!
JOHN McCAIN MADE A SERIOUS PRIMARY BID OUT OF COURTING VOTERS FROM OTHER PARTIES...
I INVITE EVERYONE TO JOIN US!
NOW GEORGE W. BUSH IS MAKING A CAMPAIGN OUT OF SWIPING ISSUES FROM THE DEMOCRATS...
EDUCATION AND FREE TRIGGER LOCKS FOR ALL!
IT'S ALL PART OF...
PARTY-HOPPING POLITICS
STRATEGISTS HAVE THE POST-PRIMARY SEASON PLAN FIGURED OUT...
YOU'VE ALREADY GOT THE NOMINATION CLINCHED...
SO START COMPROMISING YOUR POSITIONS NOW!
STRANGELY, VOTERS SEEM SUPPORTIVE OF THIS STRATEGY...
I ENDORSE EVERYTHING ON THE OPPOSING PARTY'S PLATFORM!
THAT'S THE KIND OF ELECTABLE CANDIDATE I LIKE!
SOON CAMPAIGNS WILL HAVE TOTALLY EVOLVED...
SMITH 2008
IF YOU WANT TO BE A DEMOCRATIC PARTY CONTENDER, YOU'LL NEED TO COURT THE PRO-LIFE, PRO-GUN ELECTORATE PRONTO!
...WHICH SHOULD MAKE FOR INTERESTING ELECTIONS.
THE HIGH TURNOUT OF DEMOCRATS AT THE POLLS...
...HAS LED TO LANDSLIDE WINS FOR REPUBLICANS IN CONGRESS AND THE WHITE HOUSE!
NEWS
ELECTION 2012

Stephanie McMillan

This up-and-coming artist practices what she preaches

At 37, Stephanie McMillan is one of alternative political cartooning's up-and-coming talents. Though she shares formatic and stylistic tendencies with more established artists in the genre, McMillan's approach is unique in its muscularity and striking visual appeal, as well as its focus on often-ignored and international topics. She graduated with a BFA in Animation from NYU in 1987 with an award for her student animated film. McMillan has been involved in the anti-war, abortion clinic defense and immigrant-rights movements, experiences that inspired her desire to use cartooning as a vehicle for social change. She draws her weekly "Minimum Security" strip for various alternative publications. She works at a weekly paper in South Florida, writing calendar listings and maintaining the paper's web site. McMillan also co-edits a bilingual (English/Bangla) literary zine, *Two Eyes.*

TED RALL: One of the questions people ask me is: Why aren't there more women cartoonists? I always answer: Hell if I know. I'm a guy. Since you're a female cartoonist, please enlighten me: Why aren't there more women cartoonists?

STEPHANIE McMILLAN: I don't really know either. Perhaps it has something to do with the fact that many women who have relationships and/or children are usually over-burdened with housework and taking care of their families in addition to their jobs, and don't have time to do much else (especially something that's rarely economically productive). How much art and literature throughout history has never been created because so much of women's time is taken up with life maintenance stuff? I imagine we would have a very different culture if it weren't for that.

McMillan getting arrested at a demonstration for Mumia Abu Jamal in 1995.

MAN, ANOTHER ONE IS STILL ALIVE!

THEY DON'T GET ENOUGH TIME TO STUN THEM RIGHT.

THE SUPERVISOR WON'T STOP THE LINE. JUST CUT IT.

"IN PLANTS ALL OVER THE UNITED STATES, THIS HAPPENS ON A DAILY BASIS... IT'S OUT OF CONTROL." –LESTER FRIEDLANDER, FORMER MEAT INSPECTOR.

HEY KIDS, I BROUGHT BURGERS!

YAY!

YAY!

DON'T PULL SPIKE'S TAIL, HONEY. WE DON'T LIKE TO BE CRUEL TO ANIMALS!

Why did you name your strip "Minimum Security"?

I read about a guy who had been released from prison who remarked, "I'm still not free; I'm just in minimum security." I thought this was a perfect description of the repressive police-state atmosphere that we live under, the brainwashing, the millions of petty laws, restrictions and regulations, the institutionalized violence and degradation, the education that instills conformity, the unfulfilling work.

The phrase also refers to the anxiety resulting from the lack of emotional and economic security. Most of us experience daily harassment from numerous sources, job instability, media overload, debt, alienated relationships, deficient medical care. We're subject to corrupt politicians, malevolent social policies, and disasters resulting from corporate profiteering. We worry about who will take care of us when we're old and how our children will survive.

You're one of the few cartoonists in this book with a recent history of direct political activism—demonstrating, even getting arrested. Most of us scribblers get our political ya-yas out through our work—does that make us hypocrites, wimps or both? Or are cartoonists journalists, and therefore people who should feign objectivity?

I don't think even journalists should have to feign objectivity. Everyone has a point of view that is the foundation of what they write or say even if it isn't expressed overtly. The corporate agenda underlies mainstream news. One of the great things about political cartoons is that we don't have to hide what we really think. Informed by our basic outlook, we try to expose truths as we see them. At least we're able to be honest about that, unlike many mainstream journalists who'd be fired if they tried.

As for people whose art or writing is their main form of political activity, what's wrong with that? It's taking a stand and a whole lot better than doing nothing. Making a pointed statement or exposing injustice or helping people laugh at forces they're afraid of—this is a very valuable service that challenges people to take a deeper look at what's going on. There are a million ways to fight the system. People do need to be out in the streets, but they also need commentators and artists who cheer them on and inspire them.

It's obvious from your work that you're very interested in animal rights. Are you vegetarian? Is vegetarianism a moral imperative for those interested in reducing cruelty to animals? And if cows ran the world, wouldn't they eat us too?

Yes, I'm a vegetarian. It didn't start from a moral point of view, but from high school biology class. After dissecting a fetal pig, it grossed me out to eat muscle tissue and veins and gnaw on bones. It seemed too much like it could be my own dead arm.

Later, after reading *Diet for a Small Planet*, it became clear to me that meat production in the US is wasteful and destructive. The protein fed to cows, pigs and chickens could provide enough food for every person on the planet (if we had a different economic system, that is—since it's not profitable to give away excess food they just dump it). Cattle production is partly responsible for global warming, plus the loss of huge swaths of rainforest.

I don't really think in terms of animal "rights," because that assumes that someone has the authority to grant those rights. I think human beings should just stop interfering so much with the natural world, stop thinking of it as a collection of "exploitable resources" and try to live, instead, in harmony with it. That would be better for all living things, including us. Maybe at that point nobody would want to eat sentient beings any more, or pave over ground for that matter, or drill for oil, or use another person for personal gain.

To me, the meat-eating issue is a matter of deciding what our standards of behavior should be. The current form of meat production is degrading, not only to the earth and other creatures, but to ourselves as well. We hide from the reality of the suffering, from the filth and disease of the factory farms. We should at least be honest about what we do. What makes me really mad is hypocrisy. Many people say they "love" animals, have affectionate relationships with their pets and spend fortunes on vet bills, and then deny the cruelty they're perpetuating when they eat other animals. Also, many people spend a lot of energy on the well-being of their pets or fighting for "animal rights" while ignoring the suffering of other human beings.

My favorite aspect of your work is your ability to riff on stories other cartoonists either can't or won't touch. For example, your piece about corporations patenting strains of vegetables grown overseas so they force the farmers who developed it in the first place to pay for their use is brilliant. But when my wife and I discussed the very same topic, she suggested that I do something about it and as angry as I was about this obscene practice I just couldn't summon up my muse. Do you purposely search out and focus on these—from a political cartoon standpoint—obscure topics, or is it just stuff you happen to care about?

The topics I choose for cartoons are the things that make me the most upset or angry. Oppressive practices occurring in Asia or Latin America or anywhere else are just as important to me as what's happening here. A lot of those practices are generated here anyway. Those of us who live here need to examine and address what the US is doing around the world. I have friends from several different countries, and sometimes they talk about what's going on where they're from, and things they've experienced or seen. I suppose that makes the problems more personal, which might make them easier for me to express in a cartoon.

I wrote a column applauding the Seattle WTO protesters for breaking those windows at Starbucks and Niketown. You wouldn't believe the hate mail I got, mostly from '60's-era leftists deriding violence. "Violence never solves anything," they wrote. Are they right?

What violence? You can't be violent against an inanimate object. Does glass bleed? The stereotype of violence that is pushed by corporate media is simplistic and serves the powers that be. I wonder if those critics are as con-

McMillan with Egyptian feminist writer
Nawal el Saadawi, in 1999.

cerned about the way the police sprayed
tear gas in demonstrators' faces, shot them
with rubber bullets and beat them with
nightsticks. Those who whine about vandal-
ism against storefronts should open their
eyes to the ongoing violence perpetrated on
the human race in the service of profit. Do
they get just as outraged about the system-
atic starvation of much of the population?
The 40,000 children who die each day of
preventable diseases caused by poverty? Do
those critics care that the majority of
humanity doesn't have decent drinking
water? Do they really think a Starbucks win-
dow is more important? Whenever people
strike back at the system in any way, the system cries "violence," and puts out a lot of
propaganda to that effect. Unfortunately
some people just parrot what they hear on
TV. Even when real violence is used against
people, this must be analyzed in context.
The violence of dominant economic/politi-
cal interests using police forces and armies
to crush the lives and dreams of human
beings is not the same as the violence the
oppressed use to try to liberate themselves.
The violence of resistance and revolution
may be necessary to end a greater violence.
The alternative is to leave things as they are,
because the rulers are not going to give up
their privileged position just by being asked
politely. When people start to challenge the
system, the state takes off its gloves. It's dis-
respectful of those struggling for a better
world to tell them not to fight back.

**Most Americans oppose "free trade" agree-
ments like NAFTA and the march toward
globalization for obvious reasons-they
slash American wages and encourage pollution. Why then, do you think, is there no
political will to put the brakes on unfet-
tered, unregulated corporatism?**

Do you mean political will on the part of the
dominant political parties? They will never
put the brakes on corporations because the
function of both parties is to facilitate the
growth of capital. They don't care what

ordinary people think or want. The Republicans are more open about that fact while the Democrats occasionally pay some lip service to the "will of the people." They're all lap dogs of the big corporations and will always seek to serve them at our expense.

Are Republican voters evil, misguided, stupid, or all of the above?

Democrats are easier to figure out—they harbor the illusion that their party actually stands for what it says, and think that if capitalism could just be reformed a little bit then everything would be fine. I have a hard time understanding Republicans, though. Some seem stupid and brainwashed, some willfully selfish and mean. Some seem on the surface like pleasant folks and I wonder what's going on in their heads. Maybe they really believe that promoting business interests helps the world? Maybe they fear losing their privileged way of life and think aggression is the only way to preserve it? Maybe they feel so helpless that they need powerful leaders to look up to? It's puzzling.

Are there any political points of view that you hold that could be called conservative?

I'm kind of stuffy and moralistic, which I suppose could be called "conservative" if you're a fun-loving liberal, but I consider my views progressive. We're presented with the choice of being either "conservative" or "liberal" as if these were opposites, but neither of these categories really challenges the status quo. It's like being given a choice of Coke or Pepsi. We're supposed to choose among the mainstream political parties, and any other options are left out of the equation. Once in a while, they'll throw in a Ralph Nader type to siphon off discontent (Jolt Cola). The progressive outlook

McMillan's wedding day, in Bangladesh, 2000, with her husband, his parents and sisters.

rejects all that, in favor of restructuring the whole society in the interests of the people.

Do you believe in God?

No. The concept of god—which was invented as a way to explain natural phenomena—is one of the most destructive forces in the world. Under capitalism, people are presented with the non-choice of hedonism or religion. People who don't like the emptiness of hedonism are encouraged to find meaning and purpose in a god, instead of in realistically addressing social problems. We're supposed to lie back and let god handle everything — how disempowering. And how convenient to justify atrocities in the name of god's will.

All politics is local, but you do cartoons about local issues in foreign countries like Afghanistan and Colombia. Do you get good reactions to those cartoons? Also, have you visited many of the nations about which you do cartoons?

Most of my cartoons that tackle issues in other countries point to the ways that the US is messing with them (like the US military offensive in Columbia, and US media's diminishing of the importance of what's happened to women in Afghanistan). I do get good feedback from these cartoons. Some magazines will put them with an article about the same issue, sort of like an illustration. I haven't traveled to all those places. I've been to Germany to visit my relatives (most recently about 18 years ago), and last year I went to Bangladesh to get married and meet my in-laws. I saw the

reality of much of what I'd read about, in terms of how the economies of certain countries are sucked dry by international capital. It had been kind of abstract before, but now I can see some of the ways my own relatives are affected.

Do you boycott products by certain corporations and if so which ones? Why not others?

Good question. I respect people's boycotts, like the ones against grapes or Coors beer from some years back, and avoid consuming products that I know people are actively organizing against. It's sort of on the same ethical level, to me, of not crossing a picket line. But I've never worked on a boycott. Exploitation is inherent in the production of all consumer goods under capitalism as you've implied in your question, and we can't avoid buying everything. It's all tainted. I'm not willing to grow all my own food and weave my own cloth right now; I wouldn't have time for anything else. I don't buy a lot of stuff I don't need anyway so avoiding Taco Bell or Nike is kind of natural for me, and not a hardship. But changing society isn't about what brand of stuff we consume or don't consume. My main identity is not "consumer," so I don't believe my power to affect things exists mainly in the marketplace.

Should CEOs earn more than janitors?

They should earn less because they don't work as hard. How about collectivizing the company and giving everyone the opportunity to run it and take turns cleaning out the wastebaskets?

A young McMillan expresses her dissent from Santaism.

Mickey Siporin

His "America Outta Line" chronicles the decline of Western civilization

Upper Montclair, New Jersey's Mickey Siporin updates the avant-garde aesthetic of the '60's to our own bitter age, making him one of the country's most unjustly underexposed political cartoonists. Siporin, 61, deconstructs narrative form and comics conventions to comment on social systems in work that runs in *The Los Angeles Times, Funny Times, Z Magazine, Newark Star-Ledger* and Manhattan's *The Westsider*. He is a Professor of Fine Arts at Montclair State University as well as a film maker whose work has aired on Cinemax, HBO and PBS.

TED RALL: How long have you been cartooning, and has your work always been political?

MICKEY SIPORIN: When I was about nine years old (in 1949), my brother Tom and I created a newspaper which we executed in pencil on paper. In the newspaper, which included articles about such matters as the family dog, I drew several incomprehensible "daily" type comic strips.

In high school, I did a weekly cartoon and was the art editor. At Southern Illinois University in the early 1960's, I did three cartoons a week for *The Daily Egyptian* and for a while was actually on a journalism assistantship. After leaving Carbondale in 1964 and while in graduate school in the motion picture division at UCLA, I did some work for *The Daily Bruin*.

While at UCLA, I noted a new publication entitled the *LA Free Press* on the newsstands. I became a regular contributor to this publication which was modeled after *The Village Voice* in New York City. I had work published in the *Free Press* from 1964 through 1967. As a kid, I read comic strips like "Peanuts," "Li'l Abner," "Louie," "Pogo," "Little Lulu," Disney Comics, "Dick Tracy," "Smokey Stover," and comic book titles such as *The Lone Ranger, Batman, Superman* and most importantly the first *Mad* comics.

My father was, and still is, a very politically minded person and I was privileged to experience his reactions to the news of the day as he read the *Chicago Daily News* during the week and *The Chicago Tribune* and *Sun-Times* on Sundays. He did not read the Hearst-owned *Herald-American*

Not just another Beatle: Siporin, right, protesting the Vietnam War.

and so I didn't know any of the cartoons from that paper. We also religiously watched the evening television news every night, and discussing the days' events was part of the fabric of a typical evening . Also around the house I might find publications such as *Time* and *The New Republic.*

I was an avid reader as a kid and found the works of Robert Benchley of great interest and am certain that his sensibilities have been of guidance to my approach to writing and developing comic and satirical ideas.

While I was growing up in the late 1940's, the political cartoons that I saw related more to Thomas Nast than to the type of work that I am currently doing. For some reason I never found the political cartoon on the editorial page particularly compelling and I was never motivated to work in that manner. Even when I was doing cartoons in the early 1960's that were of a political and social nature, I didn't think of myself as a political cartoonist, I thought

©1995 mickey Siporin

we're not abandoning the social safety net

we're using it more creatively.....

...restraints for the elderly

creative use # 827927138

of myself as an observer or social commentator. I think that was the view of other people as well.

During the 1970's and 1980's I was working mostly as an independent filmmaker, teaching and cartooning on a freelance basis for various publications including *The New York Times, Soho News* and occasionally doing non-political work. But, even while contributing monthly for ten years to the *Filmmaker's Newsletter* film magazine, my cartoons might reference social and political concerns.

How did you develop your highly representative graphic approach? Do you think that the uniqueness of your style has created a barrier to greater popularity?

My style of drawing and graphic ideas are the product of multiple influences which I imagine begin with my environment as a child. My grandmother Jennie Siporin, who lived in an apartment across the street from my folks' apartment was, a "primitive" painter influenced by Marc Chagall. My uncle Mitchell Siporin was a successful Social Realist painter and my aunt Shoshannah was also an artist whose work I saw regularly. Works by these family members hung on our walls and I often had the opportunity to see their paintings going through the various stages of creation. I studied art, design and art history in high school and at college; and the work of 19th and 20th

century artists have influenced my visual thinking. I particularly admire simplicity and directness in art, in drawing and in living (note I said "admire"). I do try to keep my work simple and direct.

I think it is fair to say that my drawing ideas come from those sources and the work of Picasso, Matisse, Grosz, Steinberg, Herriman, Feiffer, Egyptian wall paintings and Japanese woodcuts, the Surrealists and Dadaists, painting and calligraphy. It is important to me that I draw in a manner that is original and unique. I think this is reflected in the

variety of ways I have approached my work and a criticism that I have encountered on a few occasions.

I think that it is important to mention the influence of my film work on my cartoon work and vice versa. I have always leaned toward the multi-panel cartoon and comic strip approach as opposed to the single frame. Obviously this closely parallels film storyboard thinking. My film work has often been in very short formats from one-minute, two-minute, to six-minute bits and on occasion longer but usually even in the longer formats built around very short sequences and closely resembling the cartoon formats that I use.

Aside from your cartoons, you're also a college professor. Does exposure to young people help keep you fresh?

It doesn't hurt. It also makes me aware of the fact that each generation needs to learn many of the same and seemingly obvious life lessons that aren't offered in the educational curriculum. It's these kinds of eternal issues that we daily must confront and struggle with that I try to make the focus of my work.

What materials do you use to produce your work? What's your process?

Some odd form of osmosis. I read *The New York Times* every day, watch TV news, read a variety of magazines and then sit down with paper and an Ebony pencil and start writing and drawing.

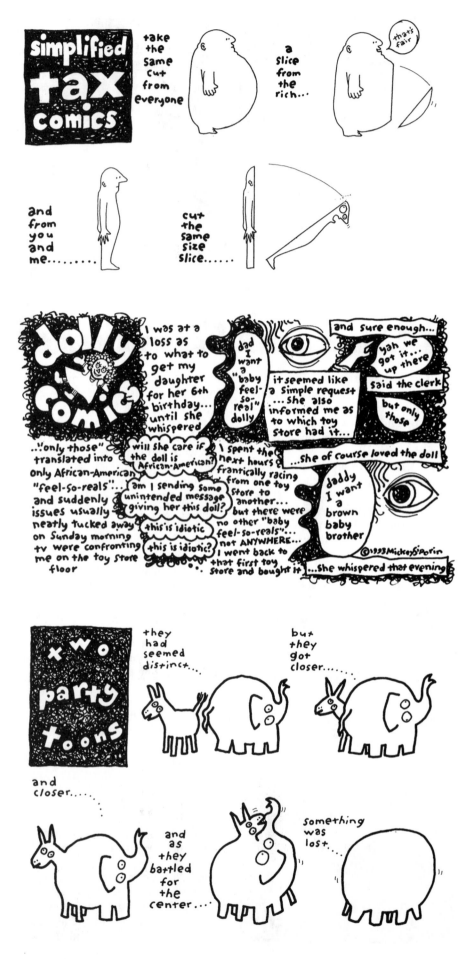

Ideas don't seem to develop until I commit something to paper. Sometimes, it's the drawing that is important, but most often it seems to be the words. I try to capture the spirit of the "rough" drawing in my final version, as I often am most pleased with my quick and intuitive drawings as opposed to my more premeditated tendencies. I can work for hours on versions that keep changing even past the final inking. I have done cartoons that have gone through 10 to 15 "rough" variations before I was satisfied. Satisfaction with an idea often comes with a real recognition that "That's it!" It often feels like sculpture on a small scale, more like whittling, as the idea is slowly defined, focused, reworked and refined. Cartoons take a minimum of two hours to six hours depending on complexity, ink smears and luck.

I currently use a Rapidograph-type pen on Bristol board, white correction tape and the Xerox machine when appropriate. I have in the past been a big fan of the crowquill pen and on occasion have used rubber stamps (and Xerox copies in the same manner).

Are all politics truly personal, or is that just a stupid expression?

I know that my work, when it is motivated by conviction or by my personal response to a political and/or social circumstance, is the most satisfying (and often the easiest to create). My politics come from the sense of social justice and idealism that I learned as a child from my family and which became better informed later in life from various experiences that more clearly focused and defined that sensibility.

Certainly my environments, growing up on the South Side of Chicago and going to inner-city schools (before there was an acknowledgment of their detrimental outcomes) and very consciously and conscientiously living through and participating in various civil rights (in Chicago and southern Illinois) and anti-war activities (in western Illinois, Chicago and New York City) helped mold my political and social ideas. Being the product of a marriage between a father raised in the Jewish culture and a mother raised as a Polish Catholic, I, at an early age, was confronted with issues dealing with religion, discrimination and ethnic identity.

What's the best educational preparation for a political cartoonist—art

school, history, politics, something else?

All of the above. None of the above. Some of the above. I believe any of the above mentioned would be useful, but cartooning might also be seen as folk art, that is guided by political and social intuition, in which case common sense would suffice.

I'm constantly astonished at the fact that your work isn't distributed far more widely than it is. To what do you attribute this fact? Is it just that you are too mellow to market yourself?

Thanks for the compliment. I don't really have an answer. But, as to "too mellow", I don't think that's the reason. Back in the early 1980's for instance, I did a strip for a major magazine and when the publisher insisted on it being a work-for-hire depriving me of the copyright, I protested and the deal fell through. Three of these full page "relationship" strips were delivered and a check was sent to me indicating that the strip which I had created was a "work for hire" if I signed the check. I insisted on receiving ownership and copyright of the strip and after waiting to hear from "Hef" [Hugh Hefner, who publishes *Playboy*] I was directed to "buzz off," thus ending that aspect of my cartooning career.

For a time during the '90's you were syndicated by the late, lamented Chronicle Features. What happened? Which publications are your natural marketplace?

The part of the question that I have a handle on is which publications. Over the years it has been start-ups like the *LA Free Press*, *The Soho News* and off-beat sources like *Funny Times*, *Z Magazine* and publications like my own *Westsider* which are open to non-mainstream ideas and art. This has, on occasion, included some happy major moments in such forums as the *New York Times*, the *Los Angeles Times*, *Toronto Star*, *Newark Star-Ledger* and *The Village Voice*. As to your question about Chronicle Features and what happened... the answer, unfortunately, was that nothing happened.

What makes for better cartooning, depression or joy?

Somehow, when I'm involved in the

Mickey Siporin

process I don't think it matters. It's a question of focus. When I'm interested in committing myself to a graphic idea, that creates a kind of joy in me so that what may or may not be going on in my personal life becomes rather important at the time I'm working. I get lost in the work. When it's over, delivered, faxed and Fedexed then reality sets in and the mood *du jour* takes over.

What kind of music do you listen to while you draw?

Today I like classical music as I am developing my ideas (Bach, Chopin, Schubert and Mozart). When I'm drawing, I'm all over the place with folks like Bob Wills, Hank Williams, Kitty Wells (country and country swing), Muddy Waters, Otis Rush, Shakey Jake, Smokey Hogg (blues), Benny Goodman, Duke Ellington, Charlie Parker, Charlie Mingus, Zoot Simms, Lennie Tristano (jazz), Otis Redding, the Rolling Stones, Al Green (rock/soul/rhythm and blues) and sometimes various folk musicians American and otherwise. Sometimes, I draw to classical music as well. I love music. For my own enjoyment, I have played folk music, country and blues since I was a teen-ager.

Is it too late to stop global warming?

I hope not.

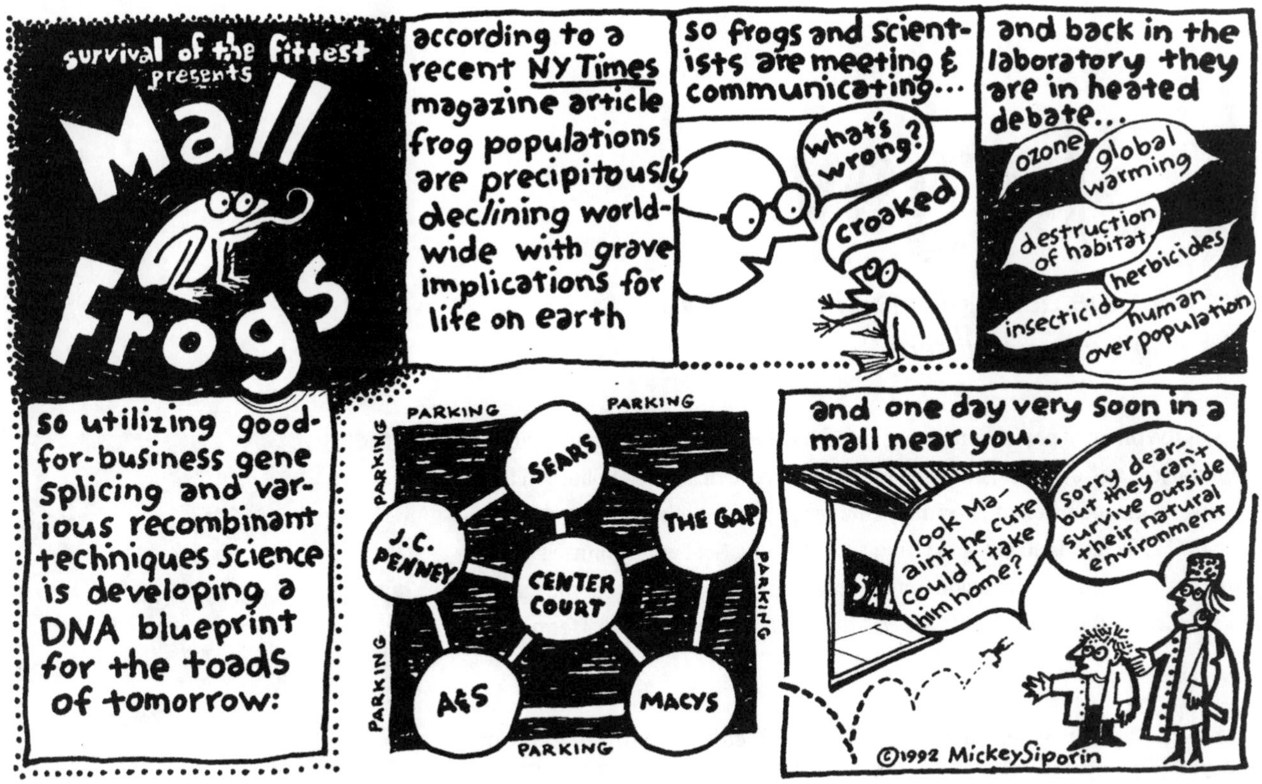
survival of the fittest presents
Mall Frogs
according to a recent NY Times magazine article frog populations are precipitously declining world-wide with grave implications for life on earth
so frogs and scientists are meeting & communicating...
what's wrong?
croaked
and back in the laboratory they are in heated debate...
ozone
global warming
destruction of habitat
herbicides
insecticide
human over population
so utilizing good-for-business gene splicing and various recombinant techniques Science is developing a DNA blueprint for the toads of tomorrow:
PARKING
PARKING
SEARS
THE GAP
J.C. PENNEY
CENTER COURT
A&S
MACYS
PARKING
PARKING
PARKING
PARKING
and one day very soon in a mall near you...
look Ma-ain't he cute could I take him home?
Sorry dear-but they can't survive outside their natural environment
©1992 MickeySiporin

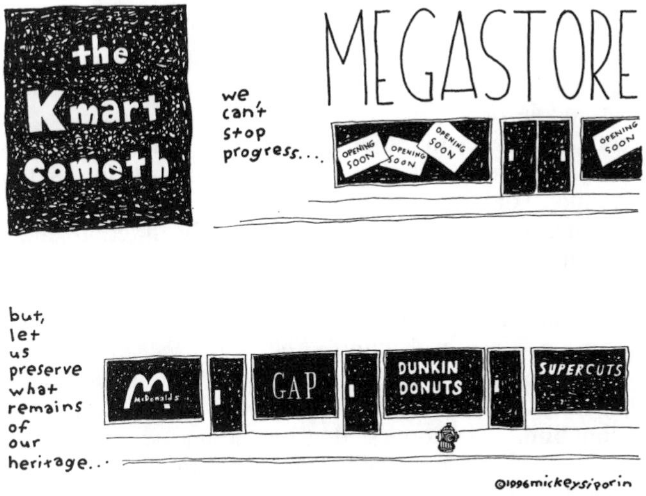
the Kmart cometh
we can't stop progress...
MEGASTORE
OPENING SOON
OPENING SOON
OPENING SOON
OPENING SOON
but, let us preserve what remains of our heritage...
McDonald's
GAP
DUNKIN DONUTS
SUPERCUTS
©1996mickeysiporin

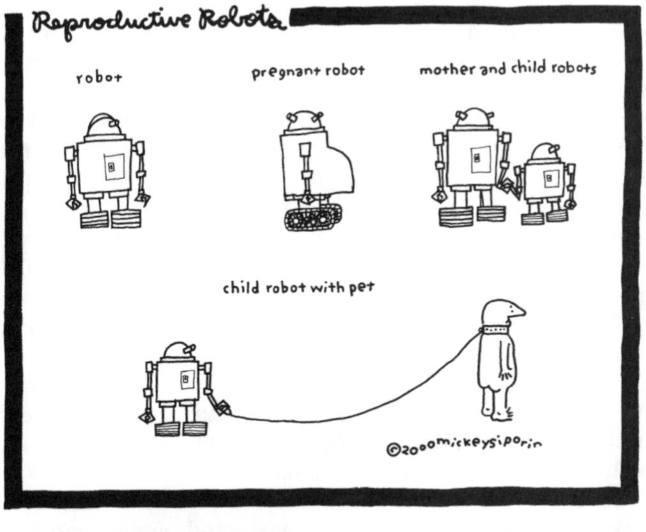
Reproductive Robots
robot
pregnant robot
mother and child robots
child robot with pet
©2000mickeysiporin

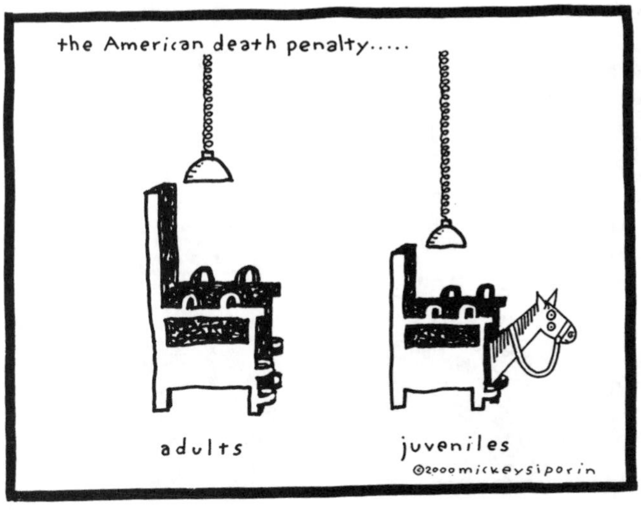
the American death penalty.....
adults
juveniles
©2000mickeysiporin

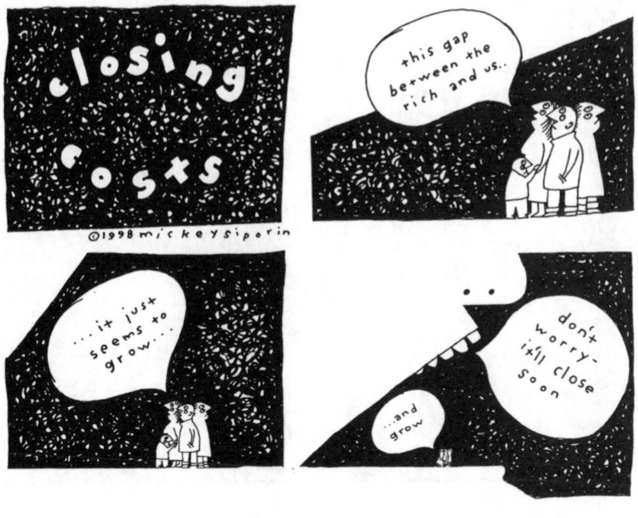
closing costs
©1998mickeysiporin
this gap between the rich and us..
...it just seems to grow...
don't worry-it'll close soon
...and grow

Jim Siergey

A few years after the death of one of its creators, "Cultural Jet Lag" is more vibrant than ever

Jim Siergey uses the prism of pop culture to magnify the foibles of politicians and regular folks in "Cultural Jet Lag," a cartoon that itself mimicks the American sociopolitical diaspora by appearing in one mainstream *Time* magazine version and another marketed to alternative weeklies. Now 52, Siergey is adapting to writing and drawing "Jet Lag" by himself after the recent death of his partner Tom Roberts. Aside from his high-profile gig with *Time*, you can find this Chicagoan's strip in *Funny Times, Comic Relief, Northwest Comic News* and *Metro Pulse* in Knoxville.

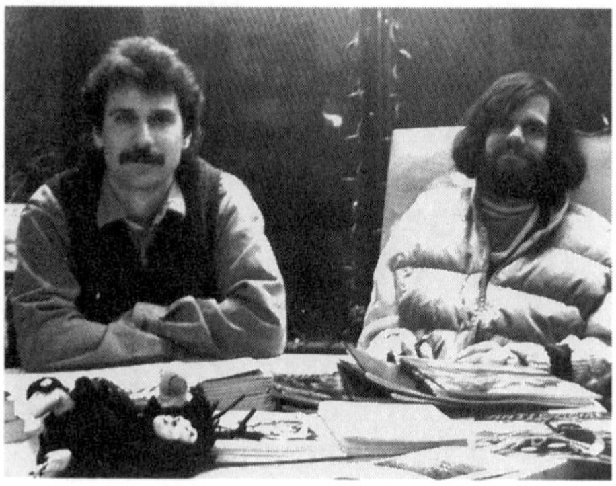

The only known photo of Siergey with Tom Roberts, co-creators of "Cultural Jet Lag." The scene is a book signing at Quimby's, in 1992.

TED RALL: How did "Cultural Jet Lag" originate? Did you do cartooning work that predates it?

JIM SIERGEY: Years ago I did an eight-page mini-comic called "Waiting for Gummo." In this book, I drew the Marx Brothers acting the parts and mouthing the lines from Samuel Beckett's "Waiting for Godot." I had always wanted to stage a version of Godot with Marx Brothers impersonators playing the roles but figured this would be the closest I'd ever get to it. (I think the two blend marvelously well.) I did this about the same time that I was sitting in on an animation class, which is where I first met Tom Roberts. He dug this juxtaposition of art forms that I did and eventually wrote a script for "Jason and the Suburbanauts," an updated version of the Greek myth that I illustrated. We started collaborating on different things and realized that we both liked melding "high culture" with "low culture." So we decided to mate in the creative sense and the warped offspring was "Cultural Jet Lag."

Before that, yes, I did do cartooning work to a small degree. Actually, I have always drawn but it was mainly for my own amusement. I did work up a couple of comic strips, "Waldo & Emerson" and "Kat Mandu." They saw print in a few places but didn't really excite anyone very much. I did some illustration work on a freelance basis but not much. Actually, after sitting in on this animation class where I met Tom, I ended up making a decent living as an animator for many years.

You used to produce the strip jointly with Tom Roberts. Tell me more about him.

I don't toss this term about loosely but I, and people who knew him concur, Tom was a bit of a genius. He was an endless fount of ideas and inspiration. It was amazing. He had this ability to look at the same things we all look at but he saw them from a peculiarly different angle and from this oblique view, great satire leapt forth.

As I said, we met in an animation class at Columbia College in Chicago. Tom produced a series of self-published glossy-covered comic books called "Anti-Social Comics" that he had a modicum of success with. They were unrelentingly dark and wickedly funny. I contributed to these books and we just started hanging out more and collaborating and before

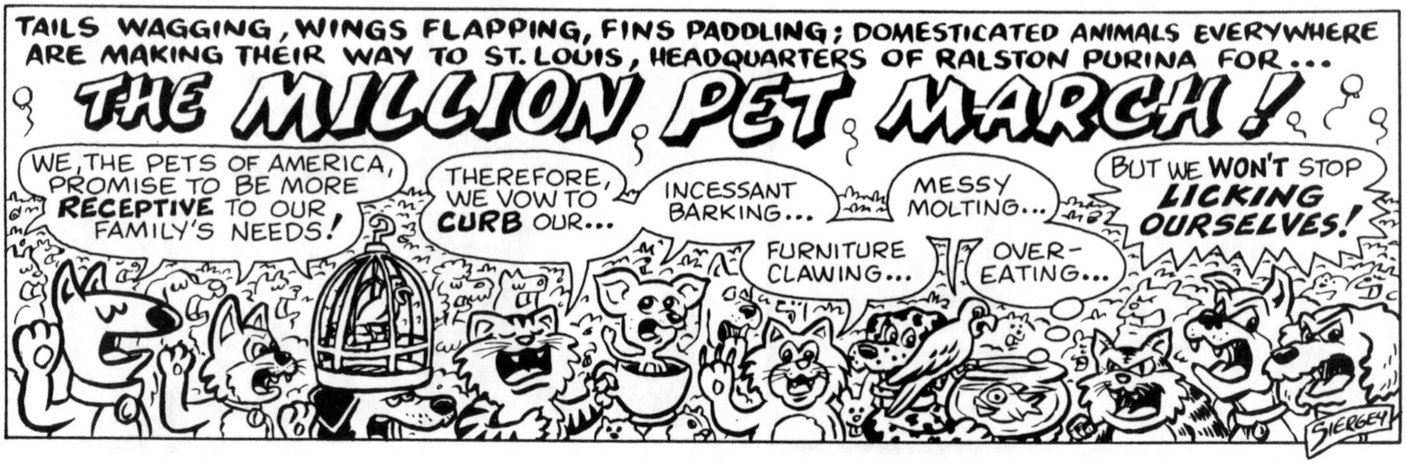
TAILS WAGGING, WINGS FLAPPING, FINS PADDLING; DOMESTICATED ANIMALS EVERYWHERE ARE MAKING THEIR WAY TO ST. LOUIS, HEADQUARTERS OF RALSTON PURINA FOR...
THE MILLION PET MARCH!
WE, THE PETS OF AMERICA, PROMISE TO BE MORE RECEPTIVE TO OUR FAMILY'S NEEDS!
THEREFORE, WE VOW TO CURB OUR...
INCESSANT BARKING...
MESSY MOLTING...
FURNITURE CLAWING...
OVER-EATING...
BUT WE WON'T STOP LICKING OURSELVES!
SIERGEY

long we came up with this "Cultural Jet Lag" concept. We started out playing with high and low culture but soon ventured into political and social commentary and satire as well. *New City*, an alternative paper in Chicago, started running "Cultural Jet Lag" and soon after that, several other papers did likewise.

Collaboration is hard to dissect. When you brainstorm together, it's difficult to remember who thought of what. Ideas tend to run into and bump off of and mesh into their own entities. This has always been my experience with collaboration, which I've done a lot of and quite enjoy doing so. It's like being Rob, Sally and Buddy in "The Dick Van Dyke Show", which always seemed to me like the greatest job ever. So, quite often Tom and I would toss ideas at one another and eventually come up with something that we could breathe life into. But, before long, Tom had so many ideas, and so many good ideas, that I deferred to him and concentrated more on being the illustrative interpreter as well as editor, since he had a tendency to get verbose.

I also played the eternal kibitzer, throwing my two cents in here and there, poking holes in any balloons that drifted into pomposity and this evolved symmetry worked swimmingly. Writingwise, Tom was Lennon and McCartney while I was George Harrison, if I may be so bold as to equate us with those golden-toned mop-tops of lore.

Tom died a few years ago. Why did you decide to continue on without him? In what way, if any, has "Cultural Jet Lag" changed?

Tom had muscular dystrophy. When I first met him he used a cane and eventually lived his life in a wheelchair. He made many a caustic remark about politics or society but I never heard him complain about his condition. He eventually developed respiratory problems and died at the age of 39 on January 5, 1999.

I had spent nine years talking and planning and trading barbs with Tom on almost a daily basis so when he expired it was kind of like going through cold Cultural Jet Lag turkey. Suddenly this strip was no longer us, it was me. A few months before he died, CJL was appearing monthly in *Time* magazine and weekly in *USA Weekend* as well as the alternative papers. Due to his illness, Tom's output had dwindled so I was scripting the topical *Time* and *Weekend* material and since we did more of the high/low culture stuff than political stuff for the alties, I had a backlog of Tom's scripts and ideas to draw from for that. (I never could keep up with his torrent of ideas). CJL had been a part of my life for so long that abruptly bringing it to a halt,

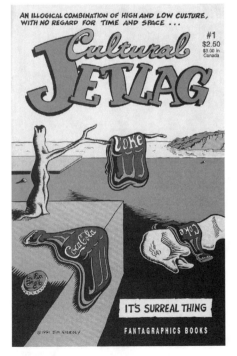

First issue of "Cultural Jet Lag."

A foray into the greeting card industry. The front of the card is above, and the inside to the right.

despite half of its creative team being gone, would not have been an easy task. Besides, Tom poured his soul into this venture so, if only out of tribute to him I felt that CJL should carry on. Plus, I still had the deal with *Time* and *USA Weekend* going and they were nice gigs. As for the alternative press, I had that folder thick with Tom's scripts that I hadn't touched yet so I figured I could use them as I weaned myself into writing on my own. As it turned out, the first half dozen strips I did were all newly scripted by me. But I have dug into that folder, and still do, once in a while.

How has it changed? Someone not as close to it as I am would better be able to comment on that. I don't think it's changed all that much. Perhaps it's less dense than it used to be. I've always tried to get a point across as minimally as I could while Tom didn't care about that. I think he had a Joycean approach to his art—that the reader should have to work just as hard as the creator did in order to "get it." I don't entirely disagree with that approach but for a comic strip to get read I feel that it has to at least look somewhat undaunting. Once you snag the reader then you can mess with his head. Tom and I shared a similar view both politically and socially and we liked playing around with different art forms and genres so that aspect of the strip hasn't changed. The strip, I think, misses Tom's special satirical bite but I'm able to leave some teeth marks as well.

The strip contains an even mixture of commentary on popular culture and contemporary politics and events. In your mind, are consumerism and American politics inextricably linked?

Do I think politicians are akin to cans of condensed milk, boxes of elbow macaroni and tubs of "I Can't Believe It's Not Butter"? Do I think political decisions are made with the use of bright colors, banner-waving and snappy slogans? Of course not! I'd be a cynic if I did.

You do a version of CJL for Time magazine. In what way, besides format, does that incarnation differ from the CJL that appears in alternative weeklies?

In *Time* magazine the edges tend to get rounded off but once in awhile they'll surprise me by what they let me get away with. It's a product of massive consumption owned by lots of stockholders so they can't afford to allow me or the other cartoonists to be too edgy or overly opinionated. (Isn't that right, Ted?) One has to be aware of who one's audience is, doesn't one? In the alternative press pretty much anything goes. Some CJL strips have peeved enough people that it got dropped from a paper or two but most editors have balls enough to stand behind what they print.

I've occasionally heard your strip criticized for its slickness. Personally, I like that—I think the commercial quality makes an interesting juxtaposition with the content—but do the critics have a point? Should jagged social and political commentary necessarily come with jagged lines?

Slickness? I've never heard my work described that way before but if that's what's being bandied about in the back rooms about me then there's nothing

left for me to do but stuff a towel in my mouth and irrigate my baby blues. I dunno, I envision how I'd like something to look and then attempt to re-create it on paper. In my estimation, I generally fail but I try my best to be clean and clear — just as I do in my personal life. (Cue halo sound effect.) I will draw in a variety of styles as I think it befits the material and sometimes it is in a "dirty" style but, generally, I guess my main style is that so-called "slick" look. What can I do? I'm a victim of soicumstances!

I like your use of the word juxtaposition because that's been a focal point of my entire approach toward life — seeing if the juxtaposition of diverse objects can coexist in an aesthetic state of grace … or denial.

Why should jagged commentary only be portrayed with jagged lines? Was not serial killer Ted Bundy a handsome, boyish-faced young man?

More than most altie cartoonists, your drawing style seems that it might lend itself to some cutesy, lucrative merchandising deals. Any luck selling out?

The Culture Vultures are a pair of opinionated carnivorous creatures who appear in CJL from time to time to critique and feast upon fading cultural figures. One of the major syndicates liked these characters but asked if we could make them something other than vultures and not have them eat people. This is how Siskel and Ebert came to be.

Is music now worse than it was when you were a kid?

TURN THAT CRAP DOWN!!

What's your favorite book? Least favorite?

Catch 22; Algebra 101.

What pisses you off—both politically and personally? Which is another way of asking: What's wrong with America?

Our avoidance of remedying the ecological havoc that has and still is being carried out upon our planet in the name of "progress," read "dollars," is a large burr in my saddle. Yes, that's right, instead of

polluting the air by driving a car I, instead, ride a horse. Flies need to eat too.

I see an ignorance or disdain of history among a great deal of this generation and I find that to be a bit frightening. Bland acceptance of the status quo, rampant incompetence and the use of ketchup on french fries also irks me to no end.

When you sit down to draw a cartoon, what are you seeking to accomplish?

The filling up of blank space with some-

thing amusing, provocative and most of all, slick.

Does cartooning ever screw up your personal life and if so how?

Personal life? What's that? As a child I was punished for drawing by both parents and teachers. In school it saved me from getting picked on or beaten up and we all know how much the chicks dig inky fingers. So, I can't say it has screwed up my life in any way except for, perhaps, the inability to take anything seriously but I don't think cartooning can be

blamed or given the credit for that.

Please tell us about losing your virginity. (And no, I hardly asked anyone else about sex.)

I didn't really lose my virginity, I just mislaid it.

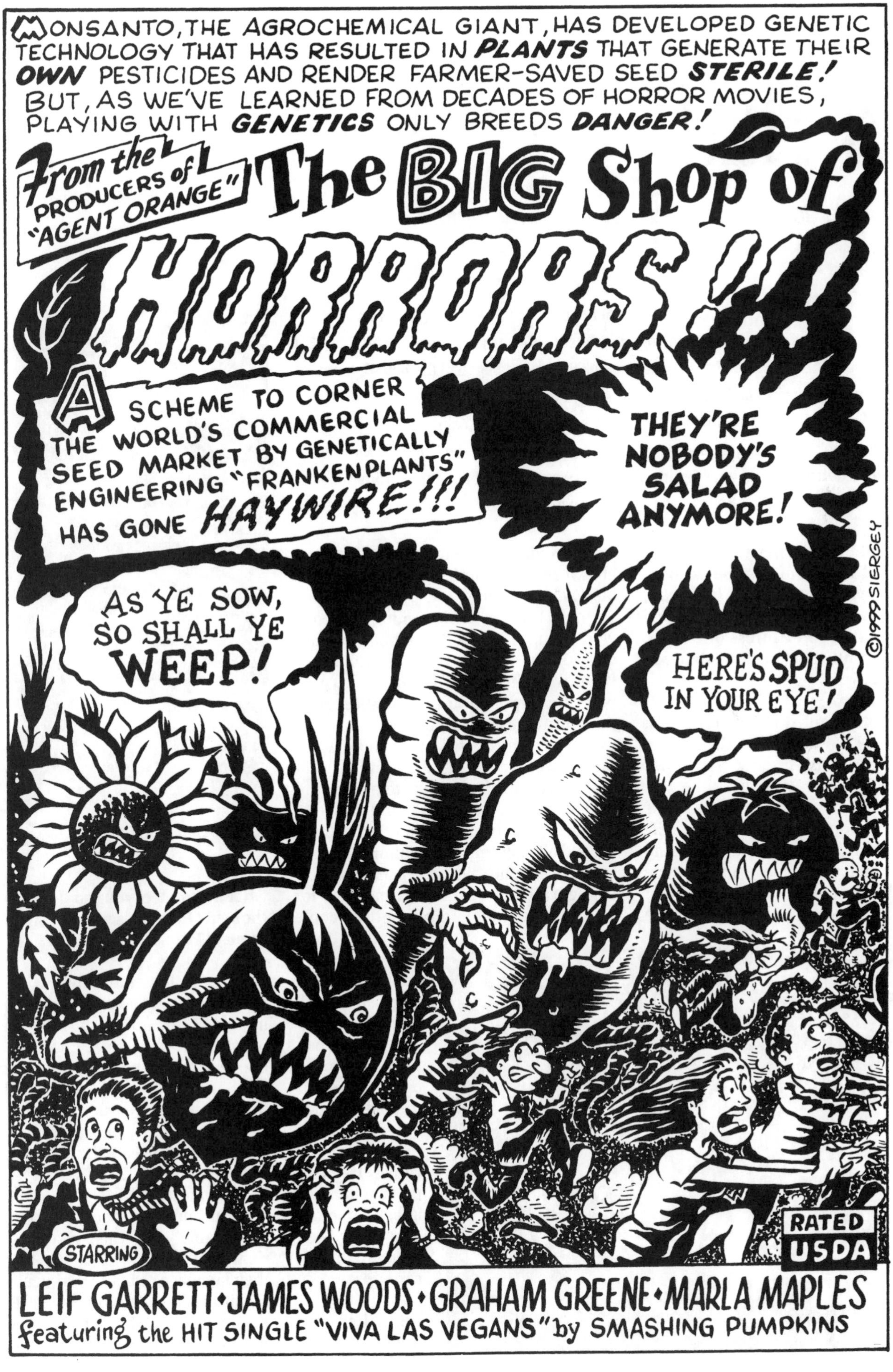
MONSANTO, THE AGROCHEMICAL GIANT, HAS DEVELOPED GENETIC TECHNOLOGY THAT HAS RESULTED IN PLANTS THAT GENERATE THEIR OWN PESTICIDES AND RENDER FARMER-SAVED SEED STERILE!
BUT, AS WE'VE LEARNED FROM DECADES OF HORROR MOVIES, PLAYING WITH GENETICS ONLY BREEDS DANGER!
From the PRODUCERS of "AGENT ORANGE"
The BIG Shop of HORRORS!!
A SCHEME TO CORNER THE WORLD'S COMMERCIAL SEED MARKET BY GENETICALLY ENGINEERING "FRANKENPLANTS" HAS GONE HAYWIRE!!!
THEY'RE NOBODY'S SALAD ANYMORE!
©1999 SIERGEY
AS YE SOW, SO SHALL YE WEEP!
HERE'S SPUD IN YOUR EYE!
RATED USDA
STARRING
LEIF GARRETT • JAMES WOODS • GRAHAM GREENE • MARLA MAPLES
featuring the HIT SINGLE "VIVA LAS VEGANS" by SMASHING PUMPKINS

Ted Rall

Cartooning's angry young man stares early middle age in the face

Ted Rall, 38, draws three cartoons per week for 140 publications via Universal Press Syndicate, roughly half of them mainstream outlets like *Time* magazine and *The New York Times*. The other half reflects his alternative weekly roots; he began in the now-defunct *NY Perspectives* and appears in *The Village Voice, Washington City Paper* and *San Diego Reader*. Known for his caustic humor and prolificity, Rall writes a weekly op-ed column and has authored seven books, including the 1998 Gen X manifesto *Revenge of the Latchkey Kids*. Because he edited *Attitude,* and interviewing yourself is weird and unbecoming, "Tom the Dancing Bug" cartoonist Ruben Bolling interviewed him for this book.

RUBEN BOLLING: You've utilized so many varied means of communication: cartooning, writing, talk radio, jazzercise, etc. Do you regard cartooning as your primary means of self-expression? If so, what is it about that medium that you find so effective?

TED RALL: I've wanted to be a cartoonist since I was a kid. When I met Mike Peters, the staff cartoonist for my hometown paper, the *Dayton Daily News,* he was hanging out in an ink-stained office behind the sports department. His wife was stuffing envelopes to send his work to his syndicated clients. In a town where most adults worked at Mead Paper, GM or the Air Force, here was a guy who'd found a

Portrait of the artist as a jailbird: age 3.

job that didn't require dressing uncomfortably. It really began like that for me, as a lifestyle aspiration.

I only became a big-mouth, someone who thought his political point-of-view was unique and interesting enough to share with the world, in college. At that point I was willing to do just about anything to express my opinions—draw cartoons, write, host a talk radio show, whatever. Having tried just about every available medium including television to express myself, however, I find that cartooning is the most consistently challenging and effective means of communication I can do. For one thing, you can never do a perfect cartoon. That brings me back for more abuse. More importantly, people who skip every word of prose on the editorial page will still read the political cartoon. They're fun to draw as well as to read. Though it's impossible to predict my career trajectory, it's hard to imagine me not drawing—or trying to draw—cartoons.

RB: When you draw a cartoon,

~SOCIETY AT A GLANCE~
LOSER   WINNER

©2001 TED RALL

what do you feel your goal is? To provoke thought? Provoke action? Change minds? Amuse? Entertain? Bewilder?

TR: First and foremost, my goal is to make my reader think about a topic or an issue in a new way. If you can cause people to question deeply-held convictions, you've opened their minds. I'm not a propagandist but that's only because I'm not good at it. If I could figure out a way to convince the American people that they should espouse income equality and put environmental concerns first, I'd do it in a heartbeat. Unfortunately, I don't know how to do that. One thing that I pride myself upon is my ability to reach conservative and right-wing readers, which I do by speaking their language rather than ridiculing them. For instance, I'm not prototypically liberal. I'm in favor of the Second Amendment [permitting gun ownership] and believe that people who are irresponsible or lazy don't deserve any government assistance whatsoever. Those stances get me in the door where my party-line liberal peers wouldn't find as welcome a reception. If I can make people smile or laugh, that's a bonus, but it's hardly a top priority for a political cartoonist worth his or her salt. My former editor Stuart Dodds, at San Francisco Chronicle Features, used to say that I had a cubist approach, by which he meant that you could come away with two or more different conclusions from the same cartoon. I'm conflicted and my work reflects that. I suspect that many of my readers feel the same way. For example, many Democrats know that their party isn't much better than the Republicans.

RB: Most other "alternative" cartoonists write and draw primarily for "alternative" newspapers and audiences. As one who has most successfully infiltrated the mainstream press, particularly the editorial pages, what resistance have you encountered with editors and readers?

TR: At first, they had serious issues with my drawing style. One editor called my work "repulsive." An editor at *The Sacramento Bee* told me that I didn't draw like an editorial cartoonist—crosshatching, donkeys and elephants, labels, tortured analogies. I replied that this is an art form, that there are no rules. Whatever works is fine, and whether my stuff works has little to do with my draw-

ing style. Eventually, mainstream editors not only got used to my drawing style, it became sought after because it was noticeably different. Nonetheless, there is still some resistance. I have never been offered a staff editorial cartooning job despite winning awards and appearing in a lot of papers through syndication. Ironically, some of the more avant-garde alternative editors consider my work too mainstream, probably because I'm actually more interested in communicating with my readers than making them scratch their heads. All I know is that I do my work and people like it or they don't.

Even if I wanted to draw for the marketplace, whatever that is, I wouldn't know how.

RB: With three cartoons a week, a weekly column, regular book output and miscellaneous gigs, how do you account for your preternatural prolificity?

TR: Fear. None of my disparate gigs pay enough to keep me in CDs and a Manhattan apartment, so I cobble together a living from several sources. If I were ever to slack off, there's a terrible danger that I'd have to go back to a day job on Wall Street. I hate wearing a suit, and I have a long history of getting fired for insubordination.

RB: Your drawing is highly stylized; did you consciously design it that way, or did it develop naturally?

TR: Both, really. I started out trying to emulate Mike Peters' heavy lines, and I've retained his playful approach involving a lot of black lines. But I realized when I was perhaps 25 that I didn't like the way my own work looked. I was drawing like a regular editorial cartoonist, but not as well since I'm not good at caricature. I started thinking about the art that I enjoy—Soviet propaganda posters from the 1920s, punk rock and New Wave album covers—and how to incorporate those sharp, geometric approaches into cartooning. Then Peter Kuper told me about scratchboard in

1986 or 1987, and that medium naturally led me to jagged angles and stylistic abstractions that I still use today, even though I've given up on scratchboard (because it's so hard to find and expensive).

RB: What's your typical way of coming up with ideas for a comic? Do they fall into your lap (e.g., while conversing with someone or catching yourself thinking about something) or do you go through some deliberate process in order to tease them out?

TR: I read lots of papers, watch TV, eavesdrop on conversations and talk a lot to my wife. Every now and then some observation about politics or society occurs to me—everyone, not just cartoonists, obviously has them all the time—and I write it down. Later I try to consider how to best convey that thought in cartoon form, and it usually just pops into my cerebral cortex. Sometimes, when things aren't coming together just right, I'll start doodling and riffing on a phrase or a notion with the hope that something brilliant results. It rarely does, but hey, you asked.

RB: Is it possible to distill into one paragraph the reason you are the angriest cartoonist in America?

TR: I actually don't think that I am an angry person; I'm very calm and rarely start anything with anybody. The difference between me and my more mainstream peers is that I'm honest about my rage and disgust. Most people try to pull their punches because their own true emotions frighten them. My personality is such that the more I repress my feelings, the tenser I become, so it's better for me and the world to vent whenever these things surface. I don't doubt that the joke-a-day editorial cartoonists in *Newsweek* are angry about the state of the world, but they're not doing their job unless they express themselves through their work.

RB: Do you ever actually get angry while writing/drawing a comic?

TR: Yes, it does happen. When I do, it makes me feel immensely powerful. The down side is that those cartoons aren't always that good. My restrained work seems to work best. I know, I know... this is in conflict with what I just said in the last question. Like I said, I'm a conflicted person.

RB: Are there topics that interest you but that you would not treat in a comic?

TR: No. I don't consider any topic, no matter how tasteless or bizarre, off-limits. This may account for my lack of mainstream acceptance.

RB: Are there topics that don't interest you, but about which you nevertheless do comics?

Depressed but thin, age 25.

TR: No. Just because something is in the news doesn't mean that one should do a cartoon about it. In fact, I often follow stories that I personally find relevant, even fascinating, but just don't make for good cartoons. Also I try to avoid doing cartoons on issues where my opinion mirrors widely-held belief. For instance, I agree with the prevalent view that abortion is disgusting yet should remain legal. What's the point of saying something that's already been said a million times when there's so much important stuff being totally ignored?

> "I've always believed that cartoonists who dish it out should be able to take it when they're criticized."

RB: You have a very highly-tuned sense of retro-aesthetics (your '66 Plymouth Barracuda, interest in antiques, etc.). How does that manifest itself in your cartooning work?

TR: In some subtle ways. Although I use a computer to shade and make other adjustments to my line art, I don't do any effects that I couldn't, or wouldn't, do manually. I think computerized cartoons, especially those with typeset text, have a tendency to look cold. (Of course, sometimes you want that effect, but that's different. Conflict rears its ugly head again.) So I'm old-school when it comes to cartoon production. I'm also interested in history, and I often make historical references in my work. But otherwise I like to think I'm moving my work into new directions stylistically. Topically, I'm far more fascinated with what comes next than what already took place.

RB: Why do you insist on the juvenile notion that there is a "correct" type of music to like—are you clinging to some high school music-nerd sense of "coolness," or is this the result of your Published Critic sensibility of absolute right/wrong judgments of art?

TR: When I was in high school, the music I liked—punk, New Wave—was anything but cool. All my friends liked AC/DC and Rush. But I remain convinced that anyone who listens to crap—like the stuff you like [Bruce Springsteen, Steely Dan], for example—would change their mind if only they'd been exposed to the good stuff. Free your musical mind and your ass will follow!

RB: How has your love of music affected your cartooning?

TR: Like most cartoonists, I listen to music while drawing. The energy permeates my work, and sometimes even affects content. Music thought it could change the world once. I don't think cartooning can change the world, but you need the illusion that it could to produce

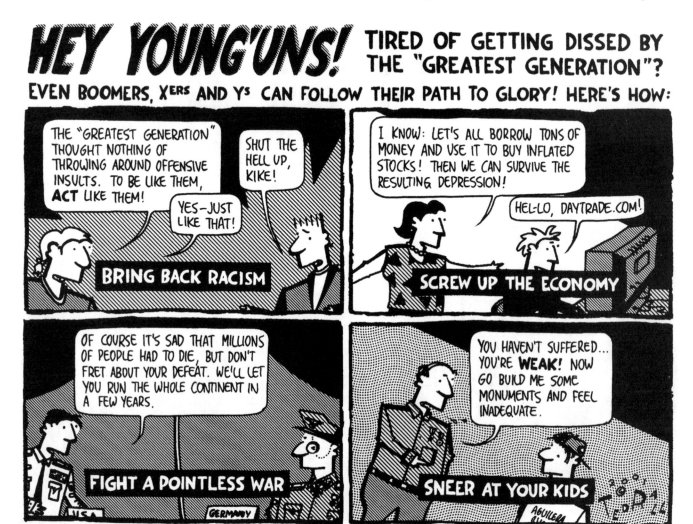

HEY YOUNG'UNS! TIRED OF GETTING DISSED BY THE "GREATEST GENERATION"?
EVEN BOOMERS, X^{ERS} AND Y^S CAN FOLLOW THEIR PATH TO GLORY! HERE'S HOW:

THE "GREATEST GENERATION" THOUGHT NOTHING OF THROWING AROUND OFFENSIVE INSULTS. TO BE LIKE THEM, **ACT** LIKE THEM!

SHUT THE HELL UP, KIKE!

YES—JUST LIKE THAT!

BRING BACK RACISM

I KNOW: LET'S ALL BORROW TONS OF MONEY AND USE IT TO BUY INFLATED STOCKS! THEN WE CAN SURVIVE THE RESULTING DEPRESSION!

HEL-LO, DAYTRADE.COM!

SCREW UP THE ECONOMY

OF COURSE IT'S SAD THAT MILLIONS OF PEOPLE HAD TO DIE, BUT DON'T FRET ABOUT YOUR DEFEAT. WE'LL LET YOU RUN THE WHOLE CONTINENT IN A FEW YEARS.

FIGHT A POINTLESS WAR

USA   GERMANY

YOU HAVEN'T SUFFERED... YOU'RE **WEAK!** NOW GO BUILD ME SOME MONUMENTS AND FEEL INADEQUATE.

SNEER AT YOUR KIDS

AGUILERA

earnest, meaningful work.

RB: While you've been very supportive of many cartoonists' work (see this book), you've also been unsparingly and outspokenly critical of many others'. Why do you think that is?

TR: I've always believed that cartoonists who dish it out should be able to take it when they're criticized. Some cartoonists are terribly smug and overrated because they receive nothing but praise. I see myself as someone out to set the record straight in these cases, just as I'm supposed to set the record straight on other issues; I know that I benefit from even the harshest criticism and I'm sure the same is true of those cartoonists whose work I've questioned.

At the same time there are a lot of artists, many of them in this book, whose work has long been underappreciated and underexposed, and it's just as important to set that straight and to give praise where little has been forthcoming. I try to do that as well. In the final analysis, it all boils down to: If you have an opinion, have an opinion. Don't be afraid to say what you really think, whether it's about the president or your best friend. The people who get angry at honest opinions are those who either know you're right or are too stupid to articulate their disagreement. Not only do I not mind someone disagreeing with me, I love a good argument and am often convinced to change my mind.

RB: Is *Dolemite* really that funny?

TR: Rudy Ray Moore, who played Dolemite in the blaxploitation films of the '70's, is a god. Start with *Dolemite*, proceed to *The Human Tornado*, and, if you're truly daring, check out *Petey Wheatstraw: The Devil's Son-in-Law*. *Avenging Disco Godfather* is only for diehard freaks, of which I am one.

On the Bishkek-Osh road, Kyrgyzstan, 2000.

Matt Wuerker

Not-so-gentle jabbing at America's soft underbelly

Matt Wuerker's first contribution to the world of American letters after graduation from college in 1979 was working in Will Vinton's animation studio in Portland, Oregon, known for its classic claymation of the "California Raisins" TV commercials. (Wuerker left before that project.) However, Wuerker, 45, quickly became known as an alternative cartooning craftsman for his cross-hatched style in his weekly strip which originated in *Willamette Week* and and moved to *LA Weekly.* In Los Angeles, he earned some extra income as a mural artist and animator for music videos — check out his Reagan-era work for Michael Jackson on VH1! Wuerker's most recent cartoon feature is "Lint Trap," which appears in such alternative weeklies as *Las Vegas Weekly, Metro Santa Cruz* and the *Washington Free Press,* as well as the *Los Angeles Times, Philadelphia Daily News* and *Christian Science Monitor.*

Still life chez Wuerker: the artist's desk.

TED RALL: Let's start with the obvious. Johnny Bench ... Daryl Strawberry ... Babe Ruth. Baseball players' names are either fake or sound fake. A lefty cartoonist named Wuerker? Pseudonym or serendipity?

MATT WUERKER: Street fighting on the burning barricades of Paris, 1968, clouds of tear gas stinging my eyes, singeing my soul, I decided right then and there to dedicate my life to class struggle. Wuerkers of the world, unite! I was never good at spelling. Just kidding. It really is my father's family name. I was just born with it. My dad, having a sense of humor, actually wanted to name me Manual. My mom, having a heart, saved me from that fate. I did have a Great Uncle Otto though. Really.

The only other cartoonist I can think of who uses your retro 19th-century cross-hatching approach is KAL, the editorial cartoonist for the *Baltimore Sun* and *The Economist.* Did you get yours from him or elsewhere?

I greatly admire KAL's work but my anachronistic notion that nicely-rendered drawing is an important part of cartooning goes back to falling in love with the cartoons of the 19th century. The virtuosity and visual humor of people like A.B. Frost, T.S. Sullivant, and Nast of course, have so much depth and innate humor that I couldn't really resist cross hatching. Later day cross-hatchers like Ron Cobb (*LA Free Press*) and Bill Plympton were also early influences.

After reading your work, I expected you to be some raving anarchist ranting about black helicopters and the conspiracy by the FBI and Tori Amos to take over the world. But in fact, you're a pretty mellow, relatively normal guy from the Pacific Northwest — I'd even trust you to cat-sit for me. How do you reconcile the anger of your work with your calm demeanor in person?

My older cartoons did have a lot of anger to them, didn't they? It's fun to get all self-righteous as a cartoonist, but I'm trying to get away from that and be a little more nuanced these days. One aspect of political cartooning that I find irritating, but is

also pretty much an unavoidable part of the job, is the need to come up with glib snap judgments about so many things that we know nothing about. It's actually not just cartoonists but as Americans living at the center of the world's one empire, we all get to do it. One week, we all have hard-and-fast opinions on how to fix things in El Salvador, the next week it's Iraq or East Timor. To bomb or not to bomb? Columbia, or was it Kosovo? I think we ought to have a three-city rule when it comes to bombing. We just hire one of those polling outfits that really run the country anyway and have them do a poll. If a majority of Americans can name three cities in whatever country that's unfortunate enough to have us fixing their problems, then maybe we are even vaguely familiar with it... otherwise maybe we should leave them alone. I don't think any of the last dozen countries we've attacked would pass this test. Serbia? Iraq? Panama? Can you name three cities? We're a pathetically bone-headed empire.

Back to your question. I think it's easy to be angry when you're younger and certain about having all the answers. I'm less certain now. The angry voice has its place and passion is a good thing, but the world has no shortage of boneheaded anger and rage. I'd like to work more on contributing more humor and humanity to life... although I have to admit that the old bile does tend to bubble up still.

You're concerned with the environment, consumerism and the increasing disparity of wealth. Do you care about issues that other cartoonists don't seem to bother with, and if so, which ones?

One that is coming into focus for me is the issue of our collective dreams. I think that marketing is the new pollution. It's robbing us of our individual and collective dreams. There is this new convergence of advertising, information technology, and our entertainment-based culture that is being employed by what is euphemistically referred to as "free market forces." It's becoming a hugely-powerful influence in our society that is effectively preventing us from hanging onto our own organic connections with our dreams, and maybe any true connection to reality. In the same way, or maybe even more insidiously, that the freemarket is taking over every corner of the world it is also taking over our minds. Many of the smartest people and

most creative talents are working for the brainwashers, using dazzling images, sex and violence to rob us of our sanity. How else do you explain our collective obsession with $150 sneakers? The way consumer culture invades every available space in carefully targeted and "synergistic" ways, the way advertising is getting married to everything from movies, TV, and the Internet, it crowds out the space that we used to have to have our own thoughts, our own desires and our own self images.

Having a kid and trying to shelter him

from these forces has been a real education for me. So many kids today are raised by these market forces. Their notion of reality, their dreams for the future, are being shaped by this culture that uses everything at their disposal to turn them into good consumers, not necessarily good citizens. In the future, I hope we will have snapped out of this and people will look back on this exploitation of kids as some sort of ruthless child molestation.

I think the same thing is actually at the heart of what's wrong with our electoral system. Focusing on the effects of money on our politics is only addressing the symptoms. Marketing politicians is the real insanity, not money. The reason that campaign financing is such an issue is because the politicians who really want to win need the money to pay the brainwashers. What sort of rational society picks its leaders based on who can buy the best pollsters and advertising agencies? Ad campaigns for elected office should be made illegal.

Call me an idealist, but I think a fair campaign would be one where all the spin doctors and brainwashers are kept out of it. Candidates should sit around a table, maybe in school uniforms—that way, no one benefits from a really good looking $3,000 Armani—and discuss the issues freely. That way, we could actually vote on the only thing that really matters in such elections: the power of people's ideas. Imagine how the last presidential campaign would have turned out if instead of the marketing circus that we were treated to, we were just given a

Illustration by Matt Wuerker

weekly round table discussion between Bush, Gore, and Nader for a couple months running up to the election. No staged rallies, no TV images with flags flowing in the sunset, no pollsters. No marketing. Bush would have been lucky to get two percent.

Your cartoon "The Codependocrats" is a sharp comment on political progressives—labor, environmentalists, gays, etc.—who stick with the Democratic Party despite repeatedly getting screwed by the "moderates" who run the joint. Should they bolt, and if so, should they withhold their votes or go the third-party route?

I don't know the answer to the "should we bolt or should we stay" question. I sometimes think the left shouldn't waste so much time on quixotic third-party efforts. I worry that we marginalize ourselves in a neat little left-wing ghetto where we're easily dismissed by the mainstream. This is not a parliamentary democracy and you win nothing by being pure and winning two or three percent in presidential campaigns.

The right made the mistake of bolting a few elections ago and hitching their wagons to Pat Robertson and Perot. They learned their lesson—they changed their strategy, rolled up their sleeves and hijacked the Republican Party. Politics is all about coalition and compromise but also about mustering real numbers on election day. If Perot can pull 20 percent and Nader can only muster two percent, it does make you wonder if the left should reconsider its approach.

You generally prefer to mock the stupid and the hateful—SUV owners, right-wingers, businessmen—rather than attack them with bitterness. Is this a conscious decision on your part?

This gets back to that anger issue. The self-righteously bitter cartoons that appear in sectarian magazines are fine if all you want to do is preach to the choir, but I believe you can reach a lot more people with humor. I really like it when I do a cartoon that gets picked up by *Z* Magazine and *The Christian Science Monitor*. When that happens you know you're getting down to the core.

Do you believe in God?

Sure.

"Sure"? How can you reply to one of the greatest mysteries of human existence and spirituality so casually?

I'm a cartoonist.

What's your favorite record of all time?

That changes week to week. Springsteen's "The Ghost of Tom Joad" is a great one. I also like Dave Brubeck's "Time Out."

You're in favor of affirmative action. But the current system often benefits, as in college admissions, well-off applicants over poor whites simply because of their skin color. Would you agree with Newt Gingrich's proposal for class-based affirmative action?

Class-based affirmative action isn't a bad idea, but only if it's added on top of a race-based approach. You can't think that 30 years of poorly-shaped affirmative action programs can even begin to counter the damage done by centuries of virulent racism and discrimination. I just love the way the right rants on about "the level playing field." It will take generations to even begin to level the playing field.

You're against NAFTA and other free-trade agreements. Are you opposed to globalization itself or just the way that an apparently inevitable process is being carried out?

Globalization is part of modern reality. How you define it is where the conflict is. Some of us think that it's civilized to provide people with water by putting up public drinking fountains. Other people think that drinking fountains need to be eliminated so as not to undercut the market for $2.00 bottled water. If you question the wisdom of this sort of market approach, the free marketeers accuse you of being against water. The globalization debate seems caught in a similar false dichotomy.

Under what circumstances would you say people are justified in using violence?

A car alarm at 3 a.m. comes to mind.

Has the Internet had any effect on your ability to sell and/or distribute your work?

It's made it easier to spread my work around to more places, but that's true for everybody out there. It's still really hard to compete with the syndicates and established editorial cartoonists. The market for independent work like mine is getting smaller and smaller and the prices people pay for reprints has been declining steadily. Mothers, don't let your kids grow up to be cartoonists—the future is looking bleak.

Describe your views on abortion.

Boy, this is going to be a really fun light-hearted interview! But continuing on in my somber, humorless cartoonist voice, choice just makes sense. Society is completely obsessed with sex. Pretty much always has been as far as I can tell. And when you then get all those free-market forces that I was talking about earlier using sex and titillation to sell us everything from beer to bubblegum, it seems preserving choice is even more important than ever.

Making babies ought to be a carefully-considered thing and not just an unintended consequence of all those Victoria's Secret catalogs, don't you think?

If you met George W. Bush in person, would you shake his hand?

Sure I'd shake his hand. I like to think when people are referring to "civil society" they're talking about our side.

Another Wuerker illustration for the cover of the great book "Corporations Are Gonna Get Your Mama."

Artist Info

Cartoonist contact information and bibliography

Lalo Alcaraz
www.cartoonista.com
www.lacucaracha.com
P.O. Box 63052
East LA, CA 90063
Latino USA: A Cartoon History, by Ilan
Stavans, 2000 (Illustrator)

Don Asmussen
asmussend@aol.com
(415) 777-7974
*The San Francisco Comic Strip:
Book of Big-Ass Mocha,* 1998

Scott Bateman
www.batemania.com
batetoon@yahoo.com

Eric Bezdek
www.ericbezdek.com
P.O. Box 465
Roseburg OR 97470

Ruben Bolling
www.tomthedancingbug.com
tomdbug@aol.com
*All I Ever Needed To Know I Learned From
My Golf-Playing Cats,* 1997
Tom the Dancing Bug, 1992

William L. Brown
www.wmlbrown.com
wmlbrown@earthlink.net
President Bill, A Graphic Epic, 1990

Clay Butler
www.sidewalkbubblegum.com
clay@claybutler.com
(831) 477-9029
P.O. Box 245
Capitola CA 95010
Hey Doug, Did You Get That E-mail I Sent,
2000
*Now This is Going to Sting a Bit So You
Might Want to Look Away,* 1998
The Glory of Capitalism, 1996

Lloyd Dangle
www.troubletown.com
www.lloyddangle.com
P.O. Box 460686
San Francisco CA 94146
Troubletown Manifestos and Stuff, 2000

Troubletown Funky Hipster Trash, 1998
Next Stop Troubletown, 1996

Derf
www.derfcity.com
derfcity@en.com
Trashed, 2002
My Friend Dahmer, 2001

Tim Eagan
www.timeagan.com
mail@timeagan.com
All-Night Comics #1, 1981
All-Night Comics #2, 1984
*The Collected Subconscious: An Anthology
of Subconscious Comics,* 1991

Peter Kuper
www.peterkuper.com
Speechless, 2001
Mind's Eye, 2000
Topsy Turvy, 2000
The System, 1997
Eye of the Beholder, 1996
World War 3: Confrontational Comics, 1995
(Co-editor)
Give It Up!, 1995
Stripped: An Unauthorized Autobiography,
1995
Wild Life, 1993-1994
ComicsTrips, 1992
Bleeding Heart, 1991
The Jungle, 1991
World War 3 Illustrated, 1989 (Co-editor)
Life and Death, 1998
New York, New York, 1987

Stephanie McMillan
www.minimumsecurity.net
steph@minimumsecurity.net
P.O. Box 460673
Fort Lauderdale FL 33346-0673

Ted Rall
www.rall.com
chet@rall.com
To Afghanistan & Back, 2002
Search and Destroy, 2001
2024: A Graphic Novel, 2001
My War With Brian, 1998
Revenge of the Latchkey Kids, 1998
Real Americans Admit: The Worst Thing I've

Ever Done!, 1996
All The Rules Have Changed, 1995
Waking Up In America, 1992

Joe Sharpnack
www.sharptoons.com
P.O. Box 3325
Iowa City IA 52244
joe@sharptoons.com
Finger Flix flip books, 2000
What America Wants America Gets, 1996

Jim Siergey
home.earthlink.net/~jetlag99
jetlag99@earthlink.net
The Culture Vultures, 1993
Cultural Jet Lag, 1991

Andy Singer
www.andysinger.com
andy@andysinger.com
CARtoons, 2001

Mickey Siporin
siporin973@aol.com

Jen Sorensen
www.slowpokecomics.com
slowpoke@virginia.edu
Slowpoke: Cafe Pompous, 2001
Slowpoke Comix #1, 1998

Ward Sutton
www.suttonimpactstudio.com
Ink Blot, 1995

Tom Tomorrow
www.thismodernworld.com
The Tom Tomorrow Treasury, 2002
When Penguins Attack!, 2000
Penguin Soup for the Soul, 1998
The Wrath of Sparky, 1996
Tune in Tomorrow, 1994
Greetings From This Modern World, 1992

J.P. Trostle
Jape@nc.rr.com
www.heraldsun.com/opinion

Matt Wuerker
www.mwuerker.com
Meanwhile in Other News..., 1998
Standing Tall in Deep Doo Doo, 1991